Scottish Mountaineering Club
District Guide Books

MUNRO'S TABLES

GENERAL EDITOR: A. C. D. SMALL

SCOTTISH MOUNTAINEERING CLUB
DISTRICT GUIDE BOOKS

Ī‌Munro's Tables

OF THE 3000-FEET MOUNTAINS OF SCOTLAND

AND OTHER TABLES OF LESSER HEIGHTS

Edited and revised by
J. C. Donaldson and Hamish M. Brown

Revision for 1984 edition by J. C. Donaldson

with a Gaelic Guide by Iain and Iseabail MacLeod

THE SCOTTISH MOUNTAINEERING TRUST
EDINBURGH

First published in Scotland in this edition 1981 by
THE SCOTTISH MOUNTAINEERING CLUB

Copyright © 1981 by The Scottish Mountaineering Club

First published 1891
Revised and republished 1921
Enlarged and republished 1933
New edition 1953
1953 edition revised 1969
First metric edition 1974
Reprinting history excluded
New edition 1981
1981 edition revised 1984

ISBN 0 907521 09 6

0907 521 096   1510

Typeset by Hugh K. Clarkson & Sons Ltd., West Calder EH55 8EQ
Printed by Brown, Son & Ferguson, Glasgow
Bound by James Gowan, Glasgow

796·522

CONTENTS

ILLUSTRATIONS

Sir Hugh T. Munro Bart., of Lindertis

Munro's Tables

ALL THE SCOTTISH MOUNTAINS
3000 FEET IN HEIGHT AND ABOVE

Revised by the Compiler, the late
Sir HUGH T. MUNRO, BART., OF LINDERTIS
and rearranged by
Mr J. GALL INGLIS, F.R.S.E.

Edited and revised by
J. C. Donaldson and Hamish M. Brown

Revision for 1984 edition by
J. C. Donaldson

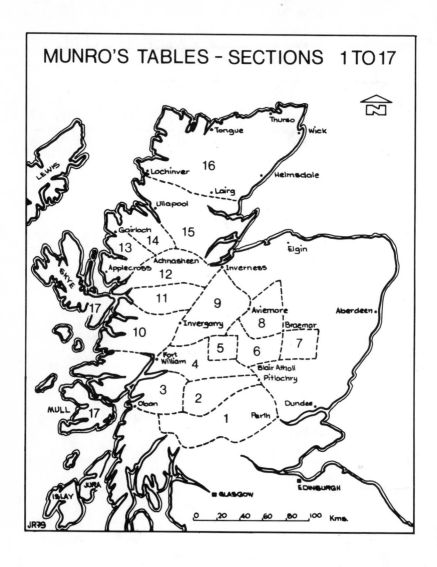

MUNRO'S TABLES - SECTIONS 1 TO 17

INTRODUCTION

THE TABLES

The original compilation of the Tables involved a tremendous amount of painstaking work at a time when little was known about the hills, and the appearance of Munro's list caused quite a stir in the then small circle of active mountaineers. Within a short time the term "Munro" was being used. The number of Munros seemed just right to make a challenge which most walkers could answer in a lifetime under the conditions of the time; many more and it would have been too onerous a task; many fewer and it would have been too easy.

Munro was working towards revised Tables when he died, so we will never know just what he would have changed. The Munros do not have a clear definition beyond the "Separate Mountain" and "Subsidiary Top" split. There is no specific re-ascent laid down as there is with Corbetts. A certain amount of "character" in a hill has affected the present revision but basically the Munros listed in this edition are the list, created by their founder, who wrote in his introduction: "the exact number cannot be determined, owing to the impossibility of deciding what should be considered distinct mountains". The years of usage have led to some changes and new maps based on more accurate surveying have produced others, and the Tables have been altered accordingly without changing the essential nature of the list.

The Editors are aware of the feelings that exist about the seemingly random or irrational nature of the selection of Mountains and Tops and they know of the arguments that have been advanced for many promotions and demotions. But if effect were to be given to all the changes proposed the Tables would no longer be "Munros". It is felt that with the coming of metrication the Tables should become an historical document and that there should be no further changes made to the list other than those made necessary when the remaining 2nd series 1:50,000 are issued. (But see the note on heights in the section "Column explanations in Table 1.) Munro acknowledged help given in his original work by Mr Colin Phillip, while footnotes in subsequent Tables and writings in the Scottish Mountaineering Club Journal through the years show the comprehensive and detailed topographical information the Club accumulated. Some of it has yet to find its way onto the O.S. maps. J. G. Inglis brought out revised Tables in 1921, reflecting many changes in the O.S. maps since 1891. Much work had also been put into this by J. R. Young and A. W. Peacock. The Corbetts and Donalds were added, both of which have been revised for this edition from the latest maps available. Changes have been made to both Tables, full details of which are given in the notes prefacing the respective groups.

The work of producing these new Tables (and the guide books to the Munros) had been held back in the hope of having the completed 2nd series 1:50,000 maps available for the areas covering Munros. However, as the few sheets remaining could be produced as late as 1990 it was felt best to proceed—and to hope that few changes would be needed then.

Hugh Thomas Munro

Munro was born in London in 1856, the son of Sir Campbell Munro of Lindertis. He was very much a Victorian figure, and dying as he did in 1919 may be said to have passed with an era. He became an original member of the Scottish Mountaineering Club when it was founded in 1889 by which time he was already a world traveller and a great walker in the hills of Scotland.

Before Sir Hugh Munro brought out his *Tables of Heights over 3000 Feet*, in the first (1891) volume of the Scottish Mountaineering Club Journal, it was generally believed that only some 30 hills were of that altitude; the authoritative Baddely's Guide, for instance, listed 31. The very first Journal had strongly hinted that the scope was far greater, possibly there were 300, not 30, "some perhaps never ascended". What could be more natural to a man like Munro than to make a tidy list of them? What could be more natural than to try to climb them all? Soon the word "Munro" appeared.

Sir Hugh was the eldest of nine children. He grew up really in two worlds, London and Scotland and as an adult he added a third, the whole world itself. When his children were old enough they went with him to Germany, Greece, Morocco, the United States, Japan, Ceylon and other lands near and far. He was a great collector as a child: fossils, eggs, butterflies and so on. Even as a young man, after a spell in South Africa, he returned with a collection of Basuto curios, antelope heads, a black boy and a monkey. He was an enthusiast with many interests all his life—a good musician and dancer for instance. He had a flow of "capital talk", no doubt like many present members of the S.M.C., though he did tend "to go on a bit" as a speaker.

His first mountain climbs were made in Germany when he was a student at Stuttgart in his late teens. He also had a business training in London. After a spell in Africa, which included serving with an irregular cavalry corps during the Basuto War, he first managed and then inherited the estate of Lindertis near Kirriemuir, which he came to regard as "home" no matter how much he wandered abroad, and his enthusiasm for the Scottish hills found its full outlet. He was the third President of the Scottish Mountaineering Club, 1894-1897. On several occasions Munro acted as King's Messenger.

Photographs of those days tend to freeze action and it was a while before shutter speeds could capture smiles. Munro was no stuffy laird but a lively and warm-hearted person; with his wide experience, talents and knowledge he enlivened any company. He would travel back from the other side of the world to attend a S.M.C. dinner or Meet. He disliked eponymous mountain names so it is a quirk of fate that his name is probably better known now than any of his contemporaries. While not a technical climber he was thoroughly capable and active, summer and winter, especially in the latter when he had more time.

Just one example to illustrate a typical Munro foray. In February 1889 he shipped to Inverie in Knoydart where the laird put him up at the lodge (he had planned to stay at the Inn). He crossed Mam Barrisdale to Skiary on Loch Hourn where he suffered the other extreme in a filthy hut which could provide little beyond oatmeal and bad whisky. He then walked up to Glen Quoich Lodge (now under Loch Quoich), lunched with the factor and had a lift to Fort Augustus. The next day he went to Drumnadrochit by steamer, through to Glen Cannich, staying overnight at Guisachan. From there he traversed Mam Sodhail and reached Shiel Inn (Loch Duich) via the Falls of Glomach. From the Inn he had a day on the Five Sisters, then crossed Mam Ratagan and Sgriol to Glenelg. The "Clansman" (steamer) took him to Glasgow and the sleeper train to London. It rather makes our car and comfort approaches seem a bit soft!

He was a great advocate and practitioner of long treks through remote areas. Often he would go alone: striding off in uniform of cape, knickerbockers (or kilt) and Balmoral bonnet, carrying a long axe and his Aneroid. Weather seldom deterred him.

There are over 80 entries in the Scottish Mountaineering Club Journal by him, many on topographical detail, for he was a whole survey in himself, and a deal more accurate than the Ordnance Survey who took another 80 years to produce reliable maps to parts of the north west. When the railways were built and motor cars invented he gladly enrolled these new fangled gadgets as an aid to exploring the hills. They were exciting days of development.

Munro never quite completed the ascent of the Munros he had listed. Carn Cloich-mhuillin above the Dee he had saved for last as it was reasonably near Lindertis and an easy ascent for a pleasant day of jollification. And then there was the Inaccessible Pinnacle, the end of many a Munroist's dreams. He was driven out from Skye by atrocious weather in 1895; in 1897 a Yachting Meet could not even anchor off Scavaig; in 1905 arrangements with Harold Raeburn (the tiger of his day) fell through. In 1906 he did the Pinnacle Ridge of Gillean, in 1908 some other Skye peaks. He was there as late as 1915 but without success.

He was past military age in 1914 but went out to work in Malta for the Red Cross and in 1918 he and two daughters organised a canteen in Tarascon in Provence. The following spring a chill developed into pneumonia and he died, aged 63.

Further information about Munro can be found in the very full obituary notice which appeared in volume 15 of the S.M.C. Journal, pages 214-219.

The Rev. A. E. Robertson was the first man to complete all the Munros (1901) and is another great figure in Scottish moutaineering.

Like Munro his talents were many and the Journal is full of both his writing and his photographs; some of the latter are superb—taken with a heavy whole-plate camera as they were! Archibald Eneas Robertson had the advantage of a Rannoch parish and was often able to take three months off at a time. In two such successive holidays he gained 72 and 75 Munros respectively. As he also climbed and had other interests besides Munros, these were special sorties really. It took what he called "a desultory campaign of about 10 years" to tick them all off.

His first hill had been Goat Fell on Arran, climbed alone, aged 12 or so, when he chose to scramble the last 1000 feet to the summit. He married twice and died in 1958 aged 88.

It is hard to picture the hills before tarred roads, railways, cars—the things which we all take for granted. A.E.R. made good use of a push bike, and a pony trap or boat would help at times, but largely he walked, like Munro, often on great through trips, finding accommodation with shepherds and keepers, for speaking their Gaelic tongue and with so many common interests, he was always a welcome guest—even when he arrived with no warning. He stayed with the McCooks at Ben Alder on many occasions—and in a note in the Journal thoroughly demolished the myth of McCook's suicide. He was meticulous in every way: good gear and careful planning, accurate observation and reporting, a fascination with history, a gift for fine photography were typical of his approach. Eye and hand made him an expert carpenter.

He was chairman of the Scottish Rights of Way Society and a Fellow of the Royal Scottish Geographical Society (as was Munro) and wrote many interesting articles on "coffin" roads and such topics. The bridge over the River Elchaig on the way to the Falls of Glomach was built as a memorial to him. He had kept the Aonach Eagach for his final Munro, an expedition he made with his wife and his oldest friend, Alexander (later Lord) Moncrieff, who humorously reported A.E.R. kissing both the Meall Dearg cairn and his wife—in that order.

A.E. Robertson was President of the Scottish Mountaineering Club from 1930-32, and was later made an Honorary Member in recognition of his prolonged service to Mountaineering.

A quite remarkable 22 years went by before there was a repeat. The slaughter of the First World War was no doubt partly to blame. The Rev. A. R. A. Burn in 1923 not only repeated the Munros but added the subsidiary Tops. J. A. Parker, Munroist number three, in 1929, added the "Furth of Scotland"—the resonant term for the 3000-ers of England, Wales and Ireland, which was coined by Maxwell who for long kept a list of those "quod eriat faciendum". With the uncertainty of the slump and high unemployment, it was a very different world to the leisured and assured one of Munro and the S.M.C. founding fathers, but just as an "explosion" was happening on the climbing scene, so a new enthusiasm was taking people into the hills generally. The Scottish Youth Hostels Association came into being. Hiking and biking flourished. It was glorious escapism for all classes. But despite this activity only eight people had done the Munros before World War II.

The thirties saw the new road to Glen Coe opened. Public transport was still freely available. Indeed, John Dow, No. 5, wrote in 1933 "the ascent of 277 Munros under modern road conditions is very far from being a feat". (How much more so 50 years later!) Dow pointed out that he was the first man to complete them without the help of a beard, and, it might be deduced from his delightful article in Vol. xx of the Journal that he considered a beard to be an artificial aid to climbing.

In 1949 Willie Docharty (No. 13) made the first "grand slam" of Munros, Tops and "Furth of Scotland", a surprisingly late date for this. Perhaps it is symptomatic of our present-day approach that only twenty five out of the first 200 Munroists have completed everything. Doing the Munros has become an immensely popular activity, made so much easier with the weekend and holiday leisure everyone now enjoys—and the common use of the car. It used to be a life-time ambition to accomplish the Munros, now it is common place—and often done much earlier in life. Like rock-climbing, it has become, if not everyone's game, at least anyone's game.

Munroist No. 4 was J. Rooke Corbett in 1930, who of course compiled (and climbed) the list of 2500 ft. summits—the post graduate course for Munroists. Most combinations have now happened. Mrs Hirst in 1947 completed the first female round, and also a husband-wife combination. The Macdonalds in 1958 saw a father-and-son Munro effort, and in 1974 there was a Lawsons father-and-son Munros and Tops success. Anne Littlejohn made "the grand slam" in 1960. In 1964 Philip Tranter did them all again, something which several people have now managed and again a reflection on the leisure time available. H. M. Brown and Kathy Murgatroyd have done them in single expeditions. The appeal still lies in their being sufficiently hard and sufficiently numerous to make it a real challenge. They may be done in a youthful romp or in a lifetime of stolen moments but the reward is the same. They are not open to competition so retain their amateur status and varied approach. The editors' only plea is to the gentler walker: do not leave the Cuillin till last! We know too many fine old friends who "have done them all, except Skye".

There are probably as many Munroists living in Sheffield and Manchester as there are in all Scotland; fortunately Scotland has the hills and England the cities from which with true dedication the English set out on the Munro trail; any long weekend or holiday sees an invasion from the south. By the time you have done all the Munros you know Scotland as few others can and you know it in all its climatic variations. (If you have driven 800 miles to climb a few hills, you climb a few hills.) Dreaming of it, planning it, packing for it, this is all part of the game. The pubs and chip shops en route, the A9 roadworks, huts, bothies and camps all become part of the game. Others may slack or funk foul weather, the Munroist goes forth to war regardless, and now and then is blessed beyond belief. The whole rich experience of the hills is his. There are rock-climbers who just climb rock. They have their reward, but the Munroist is driven, willy-nilly to a wider experience in every way. He is seldom just a Munroist.

Some people have suggested the 3000 foot altitude should be changed to the tidy 1000 metre mark. This suggestion meets with little approval. Munro's Tables would not be Munro's Tables if so emasculated. Too easy a task would remove the essential challenge. As their pursuit (and even their definition) is irrational, the historical and traditional aspects demand we keep the *status quo*. It is interesting to see that the new *metric* Bartholomew's map specifically marks Munros. (In contrast the Ordnance Survey still refuse to name some of them or give them a height though they have been with us for over 80 years.) No, a list of 3282 foot peaks would not be the Munros!

The list of people who had done the Munros which appeared in the last edition of the Tables has been continued but it is known that not every one who does all the Munros reports the fact so that the list cannot be taken as complete. The list is maintained by the Editor of the Scottish Mountaineering Club Journal but it was Eric Maxwell of the Grampian Club, Dundee, who began the catalogue. In successive issues of the Grampian Club Journal he listed "all who, to the best of the author's knowledge have climbed every Munro and, also, which of them have climbed other mountains and tops in Munro's and/or Maxwell's Tables". Maxwell did the grand slam and was the first to do the Munros and tops twice. There are notes on Munroists, usually highly entertaining and including information supplied by Maxwell, in all issues of the Scottish Mountaineering Club Journal from 1961 onwards. Many other articles on Munros and Maxwells are scattered throughout the Journals from 1890 to the present day.

Most of this biographical note is based on the similar chapter from *Hamish's Mountain Walk* (Gollancz 1978) and various stories about Munro are scattered in that account of doing all the Munros. Richard Gilbert's small book *Memorable Munros* (Advertiser Office, York) has culled various accounts as well. Campbell Steven's *The Story of Scotland's Hills* (Hale 1975) is also full of interesting history.

Editors' Notes

Munros

Throughout the life of the Tables there has been discussion on the seemingly random or irrational nature of elevation to the Munro peerage. Munro left no definition, indeed had none, so what constitutes a Munro is bound to be subjective. Strong cases have been made for many promotions and demotions but the editors have made only a few changes to remove the worst anomalies without basically altering the Tables as Munro envisaged them.

Tops

An effort has been made to rationalise these many elevations over the 3000 foot level. Many have been removed as they present an insufficient rise or definition to really merit any title. A few have been added due to changes on maps. Several double-topped summits have had their lower member enrolled as a "Top"—probably a more valid and certainly clearer use of the word "Top" than its regular employment for minor bumps which can be a long way from the summit proper.

The alterations to Munros and Tops are listed at the end of the prefatory notes.

Lay-out

This has been simplified by removing some columns and also clarified by introducing collective names for groups within the Sections which have been renumbered for more convenient use with the guide books. The maps are collected in one place. A few groups have changed their section. (For instance, the Aonach Eagach is placed with Glen Coe, not the Mamores.) The numbering of the Sections are from South to North, 1 to 9 covering the area south of the Great Glen, 10 to 16 that to the North, with 17 covering Skye and Mull as before.

Column Explanations in Table I

Column 1. Name The O.S. 2nd series 1:50,000 names/spellings are used wherever possible as this is the standard walkers' map. These names/spellings are not always correct, or there may be variations or local differences. Larger scale maps, previous editions of the Tables, or other sources have been used where the present O.S. map has not given a name. In a few cases names have been changed to conform with alterations in the O.S. maps. Names may not be given of some peaks in Bartholomew's maps, and spellings may differ. *Indicates that the name is not given in the 1:50,000 map.

Column 2. Height The O.S. 2nd series 1:50,000 heights are followed, where given. Larger scale maps or other sources have been used where heights are missing. In some cases it will be found that heights quoted in the Tables differ from those shown on 2nd series 1:50,000 maps the O.S. having already revised them. Heights marked with a † have been taken from 1:10,000 or 1:25,000 maps 3000 feet = 914.4m, which excludes Beinn Dearg (Torridon), height 2998 feet. c denotes a contour.

Columns 3 and 4. Munros/Tops. These are listed in order of altitude, the separate mountains styled Munros in column 3 and the hills without separate status, referred to as "Tops", in column 4.

Columns 5 and 6. 5 gives the number of the 2nd series 1:50,000 map(s) on which the Munros appear and 6 the numbers of the Bartholomew maps, 1:100,000 National series. Not all numbers may be given if a hill appears on more than one sheet.

Column 6. Map References. An explanation of their use appears on all O.S. 1:50,000 maps.

Maps. The following are the O.S. maps (1:50,000) required to cover the Munros:
9 15 16 19 20 25 32 33 34 35 36 40 41 42 43 44 48 50 51 52 56 57.
In the case of Bartholomew's the numbers are: 44 47 48 50 51 52 54 55 58 59 60.
Also recommended are:
S.M.C. The Black Cuillin, Island of Skye (James Renny) 1:15,000.
O.S. Outdoor Leisure Map: The Cuillin and Torridon Hills 1:25,000.
O.S. Outdoor Leisure Map: High Tops of the Cairngorms 1:25,000.

THE GEOGRAPHICAL SECTIONS

South of the Great Glen

1. The country south of a line from Oban, Dalmally, Strath Fillan, Loch Tay and on to the A9.
2. The area bounded by the West Highland railway, Loch Rannoch, the A9, Loch Tay, Glen Dochart, Strathfillan to Bridge of Orchy.
3. The area bounded by Loch Linnhe, Loch Leven, the Blackwater Reservoir, the West Highland railway, Bridge of Orchy, Tyndrum and Oban.
4. The area bounded by upper Loch Linnhe, Glen Spean, Loch Ericht, Blackwater Reservoir, Loch Leven.
5. The hills on either side of the A9 at the Drumochter Pass.
6. The area bounded by Glen Tromie, Glen Geldie, Braemar, the A93 to Perth, the A9 through Blair Atholl and the Gaick Pass.
7. The country east of the A93 Braemar-Perth road and south of the River Dee from Braemar to Aberdeen.
8. The country east and north of the Glen Feshie, Glen Geldie, Braemar-Aberdeen line.
9. The area bounded by the Great Glen, the A9 from Inverness to Newtonmore and the A86 from Newtonmore to Spean Bridge.

North of the Great Glen

10. The mainland south of Glen Shiel and Glen Moriston and West of the Great Glen.
11. The Area north of Glen Shiel and Glen Moriston, and south of Loch Mullardoch, bounded in the west by the coast, and in the east by the Great Glen.
12. The area south of the Kyle of Lochalsh—Beauly railway and north of a line from Kyle of Lochalsh—Loch Mullardoch to Cannich, with Cannich—Beauly forming the eastern boundary.
13. The area west of the Kyle of Lochalsh-Achnasheen railway and south of a line from Achnasheen to Poolewe.
14. The area north of the road from Garve through Achnasheen to Poolewe and south of the road from Garve to Loch Broom.
15. The country between the Inverness-Garve-Ullapool road and a line from Ullapool to Lairg.
16. The country north of the Lochinver-Lairg road.
17. The Islands of Mull and Skye.

Details of changes to Munros and Tops

The 1974 edition of *Munro's Tables* listed 279 Munros and 541 Tops. The corresponding numbers in this edition are 276 and 516.

Munros

Number listed in 1974	279
Add—already reported—section 12 (new numbering)	
Sgurr nan Ceannaichean	1
after revision by editors	
New Section 4 Mamores—Sgor an Iubhair	
10 Loch Nevis—Garbh Chioch Mhor	
13 Liathach—Mullach an Rathain	
14 An Teallach—Sgurr Fiona	4
	284

Deduct—already reported—Section 1 (old numbering)
    Beinn an Lochain (height 901m)   1

after revision by editors

New Section 8	Carn Cloich-mhuillin		
	Meal Dubhag		
	Carn Ban Mor		
	Geal Charn		
	A' Choinneach		
9	Monadh Liath:—		
	Carn Ban		
	Carn Ballach	7	8

                                     276

Tops
Number listed in 1974   541
Add new Tops   21

                                     562
Less Tops deleted   46

                                     516

Names of new Tops

New Section	1.	Ben Lui—North West Top.
	4.	Sgor an Iubhair—Stob Coire a' Mhail.
		Beinn na Socaich.
	7.	Creag Leacach—South West Top.
		White Mounth—Eagle's Rock.
	6.	Carn a' Chlamain—North Top, but see deletions.
	8.	Bynack More—Bynack Beg.
	10.	Meall Buidhe—South East Top.
		Luinne Bheinn—East Top.
		The Saddle:
		Trig Point
		East Top
		Sgurr na Sgine—North West Top.
	11.	Carn na Con Dhu.
	12.	An Riabhachan—North East Top (not to be confused with the Summit, shown in the 1974 edition as the North East Top).
		An Riabachan—South West Top.
		Sgurr nan Ceannaichean.
	14.	Mullach Coire Mhic Fhearchair:—
		East Top
		Sgurr Dubh.
		Slioch North Top.

Names of new Tops (continued)

New Section 14. A' Chailleach—Toman Coinich.
 17. Bla Bheinn—South West top.

Names of Tops deleted
Old Section 1. Beinn an Lochain.
 3. Carn Mairg Range:—
 Meall Luaidhe.
 Meall Buidhe—South East Top.
 Beinn Heasgarnich—Stob an Fhir Bhoga.
 4. Clach Leathad Range—Mam Coire Easain.
 5. Carn Mor Dearg—Carn Beag Dearg.
 Aonach Mor—Stob Coire an Fhir Dhuibh.
 Stob Choire Claurigh—North Top.
 Mullach Coire an Iubhair—Sron Garbh.
 6. Carn a' Chlamain—North Top.
 Carn Liath—A' Bhuidheanach.
 Carn Ban—Sneachdach Slinnean.
 8. Sgurr nan Ceathreamhnan—Creag nan Clachan Geala.
 Mullach Fraoch-choire—North East Top.
 Carn Eighe—Creag na h-Eige.
 Tigh Mor na Seilge—Munro now Sail Chaorainn and old top No. 505 deleted.
 Creag a' Choire Aird—East Top.
 Mam Sodhail:—
 Stob Coire Coulavie
 Ciste Dhubh.
 9. Sgurr na Lapaich:—
 Rubha na Spreidhe.
 Creag a' Chaorainn.
 Braigh a' Choire Bhig.
 Creag Toll a' Choin.
 10. Beinn Eighe—Creag Dhubh.
 12. Ben Wyvis—Fiaclach.
 14. Ben Avon:—
 South West Top.
 Stob Bac an Fhurain.
 Mullach Lochan nan Gabhar.
 Stuc Gharbh Mhor.
 Stob Dubh an Eas Bhig.
 Beinn a' Bhuird—A' Chioch.
 Derry Cairngorm—Little Cairngorm.
 Ben Macdui—Stob Coire Sputan Dearg.
 Cairngorm:—
 Fiacaill Coire an t-Sneachda.
 Fiacaill a' Choire Chais.
 Sron a' Cha-no.
 Creag an Leth-choin—North Top.
 Fiacaill na Leth-choin.

Names of Tops deleted (continued

Old Section	14.	Braeriach—Stob Coire an Lochain.

Mullach Clach a' Bhlair—Diollaid Coire Eindart.

15.	A' Bhuidheanach Bheag—Meall a' Chaorainn.

An Sgarsoch—Druim Sgarsoch.

Beinn Dearg—Beinn Gharbh.

Carn nan Sac.

16.	Cairn Bannoch—Creag Leachdach.

Lochnagar—Little Pap.

Finally, the editors acknowledge their indebtedness to Sir Hugh Munro and to all those who subsequently assisted with revisions of the Tables for the help this has been in preparing this new Edition. Thanks are due to those who supplied illustrations and diagrams, to D. J. Fraser for permission to include *The Lost Leader,* and especially to the staff of the National Library of Scotland for much assistance given most willingly over many days in the Map Room. Appreciation is also expressed to those who wrote to the editors about the inclusion or exclusion of a number of hills in the three sections of the Tables, and to those who have pointed out errors. All comments have been of value.

ADDENDA

Beinn Teallach, Section 9, Corbetts, 913 m. The O.S. 1 : 25000 1984 map shows the height as 915 m. The peak is therefore promoted to Munro status thus making 277 Munros with 517 Tops; Corbetts being reduced by 1.

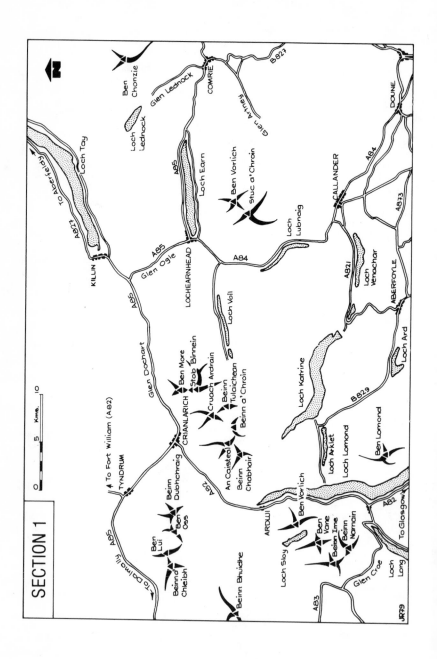

SECTION 1

Table I. Arranged according to Districts 13

TABLE 1

South of the Great Glen

SECTION 1

	NAME	Height	No. in order of Altitude Mtn.	Top	Map Sht. Nos. O.S.	Bart.	Map Reference
	BEN LOMOND and THE ARROCHAR ALPS						
1.	Ben Lomond	974	179	304	56	44/48	367029
2.	Beinn Narnain	926‡	255	467	56	48	272067
3.	Beinn Ime..................	1011	115	195	56	48	255085
4.	Ben Vane	915	274	513	56	48	278098
5.	Ben Vorlich	943	224	403	56/50	48	295123
6.	Ben Vorlich—North Top ...	931	—	445	56/50	48	294130
7.	Beinn Bhuidhe..............	948	212	383	56/50	48	204187
	TYNDRUM GROUP						
8.	Beinn a'Chleibh..........	916	273	510	50	48	251256
9.	Ben Lui (Beinn Laoigh)	1130	27	44	50	48	266263
10.	Ben Lui—North-west Top ..	1127	—	48	50	48	265264
11.	Ben Oss....................	1029	99	166	50	48	287253
12.	Beinn Dubhchraig..........	978	171	290	50	48	308255
	CRIANLARICH, BALQUHIDDER AND GLEN FALLOCH						
13.	Beinn Chabhair.............	933	243	440	50/56	48	367180
14.	An Caisteal................	995	144	243	50/56	48	379193
15.	Beinn a' Chroin............	940*	227	412	50/56	48	394186
16.	Beinn a' Chroin—West Top.	938*	—	424	50/56	48	386185
17.	Beinn Tulaichean...........	946	217	392	56	48	416196
18.	Cruach Ardrain.............	1046†	84	142	51/56	48	409211
19.	Stob Garbh...............	959††	—	354	51/56	48	411221
20.	Ben More	1174	15	25	51	48	432244
21.	Stob Binnein	1165	17	28	51	48	434226
22.	Stob Coire an Lochain	1068	—	114	51	48	438220
23.	Meall na Dige............	966	—	329	51	48	452226

‡*927m on 1:10,000 map.*
Heights shown on O.S. sheets 50/56 differ. The correct heights for Beinn a' Chroin and the West Top are as given above.
†*Landranger map. Height 1045m.*
††*Landranger map. Height 960m.*

	CRIEFF and LOCH EARN						
24.	Ben Vorlich	985	161	268	57	48	629189
25.	Stuc a' Chroin	975	176	300	57	48	617175
26.	Ben Chonzie (Ben-y-Hone) ...	931	246	444	51/52	48	773309

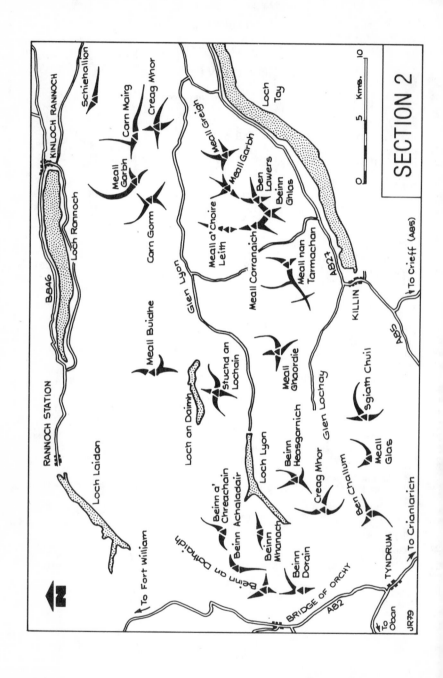

SECTION 2

Table I. Arranged according to Districts 15

SECTION 2

	NAME	Height	No. in order of Altitude Mtn.	Top	Map Sht. Nos. O.S.	Bart.	Map Reference
	RANNOCH—GLEN LYON						
1.	Schiehallion	1083	57	94	51/52	48	714548
2.	Carn Mairg.................	1041†	88	151	51	48	684513
3.	Meall Liath*..............	1012	—	194	51	48	692511
4.	Meall a' Bharr	1004	—	214	51	48	668516
5.	Creag Mhor*	981	167	279	51	48	695496
6.	Meall Garbh................	968†	182	320	51	48	646517
7.	An Sgorr*.................	924	—	476	51	48	641509
8.	Carn Gorm.................	1028†	100	168	51	48	635501
9.	Stuchd an Lochain	960	194	350	51	48	483449
10.	Sron Chona Choirein*	920c†	—	486	51	48	494446
11.	Meall Buidhe	932†	244	442	51	48	498499
	THE LAWERS GROUP						
12.	Ben Lawers................	1214	9	14	51	48	636414
13.	Creag an Fhithich*	1047	—	140	51	48	635423
14.	An Stuc*.................	1118	—	56	51	48	639430
15.	Meall Garbh................	1118	35	55	51	48	644437
16.	Meall Greigh	1001	134	223	51	48	674438
17.	Bheinn Ghlas	1103	45	76	51	48	626404
18.	Meall Corranaich	1069	65	110	51	48	616410
19.	Meall a' Choire Leith	926	257	469	51	48	612439
20.	Meall nan Tarmachan.......	1043	87	149	51	48	585390
21.	Meall Garbh*.............	1026	—	172	51	48	578383
22.	Beinn nan Eachan	1000c	—	226	51	48	569384
23.	Creag na Caillich..........	916**	—	511	51	48	563377
	MAMLORN						
24.	Meall Ghaordie	1039	90	154	51	48	514397
25.	Beinn Heasgarnich	1076	61	102	51	48	413383
26.	Creag Mhor	1048†	80	136	50	48	391361
27.	Stob nan Clach*	958	—	358	50	48	387352
28.	Ben Challum	1025	103	173	50	48	387322
29.	Ben Challum—South Top ..	997	—	239	50	48	386316
30.	Meall Glas	960 •	193	349	51	48	431322
31.	Beinn Cheathaich	937	—	429	51	48	444327
32.	Sgiath Chuil	935	238	434	51	48	463318
33.	Meall a' Churain	918	—	500	51	48	463326
	BRIDGE OF ORCHY HILLS						
34.	Beinn Dorain	1076†	62	103	50	48	326378
35.	Beinn an Dothaidh	1002	130	217	50	48	332408
36.	Beinn Achaladair..........	1039	91	155	50	48	344432
37.	Beinn Achaladair— South Top	1002	—	220	50	48	342421
38.	Beinn a' Chreachain	1081	59	98	50	48	373441
39.	Meall Buidhe	977	—	294	50	48	359439
40.	Beinn Mhanach	954	205	371	50	48	373412
41.	Beinn a' Chuirn	924	—	474	50	48	360411

• Meall Glas .Landranger 957m.
**height taken from 1:10,000

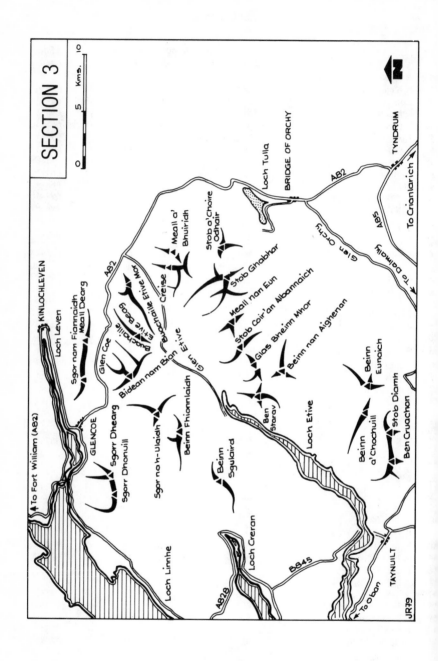

SECTION 3

Table I. Arranged according to Districts   17

SECTION 3

	NAME	Height	No. in order of Altitude Mtn.	Top	Map Sht. Nos. O.S.	Bart.	Map Reference
	CRUACHAN GROUP						
1.	Ben Cruachan	1126	31	49	50	47	069304
2.	Stob Dearg (Taynuilt Peak)*	1104†	—	74	50	47	062307
3.	Meall Cuanail	918	—	503	50	47	069295
4.	Drochaid Ghlas*	1009	—	202	50	47	083306
5.	Stob Diamh*	998	141	236	50	47	095308
6.	Stob Garbh*..............	980	—	289	50	47	095302
7.	Sron an Isean*	966	—	328	50	47	099311
8.	Beinn a' Chochuill..........	980	168	284	50	47	110328
9.	Beinn Eunaich	989	152	257	50	48/47	136328
	ETIVE HILLS						
0.	Beinn nan Aighenan	960c†	192	344	50	47/48	149405
1.	Ben Starav	1078	60	101	50	47/48	126427
2.	Meall Cruidh*	930	—	449	50	47/48	129416
3.	Stob Coire Dheirg*	1068	—	115	50	47/48	128425
4.	Glas Bheinn Mhor...........	997	142	238	50	47/48	153429
5.	Stob Coir' an Albannaich.....	1044	86	147	50	47/48	169442
6.	Meall nan Eun	928	250	455	50	47/48	192449
	THE CORRIE BA RANGE						
7.	Stob Ghabhar	1087	54	90	50	48	230455
8.	Stob a' Bhruaich Leith	939	—	421	50	47/48	208459
9.	Sron a' Ghearrain	991c	—	253	50	48	221457
0.	Sron nan Giubhas	974	—	307	50	48	231462
1.	Aonach Eagach*	991c	—	252	50	48	236454
2.	Stob a' Choire Odhair........	943	223	402	50	48	258461
3.	Creise*	1100	48	80	41	48	238507
4.	Clach Leathad	1098	—	82	50	48	240493
5.	Stob a' Ghlais Choire*	996	—	241	41	48	240516
6.	Meall a' Bhuiridh	1108	43	68	41	48	251503
	GLENCOE						
	Buachaille Etive Mor:—						
7.	Stob Dearg.................	1022	106	176	41	48	223543
8.	Stob na Doire.............	1011	—	196	41	47/48	207533
9.	Stob Coire Altruim	941†	—	411	41	47/48	197531
0.	Stob na Broige............	956†	—	365	41	47/48	191526
	Buachaille Etive Beag:—						
1.	Stob Dubh	958	197	355	41	47/48	179535
2.	Stob Coire Raineach	925	—	471	41	47/48	191548
3.	Bidean nam Bian............	1150*	23	36	41	47/48	143542
4.	Stob Coire nam Beith	1107	—	70	41	47/48	139546
5.	Stob Coire nan Lochan.....	1115	—	60	41	47/48	148549
6.	Stob Coire Sgreamhach	1072	—	106	41	47/48	155536
7.	Beinn Fhada..............	952	—	379	41	47/48	159541
	Beinn Fhada—						
8.	North-east Top	931	—	446	41	47/48	164543

SECTION 3 *(continued)*

	NAME	Height	*No. in order of Altitude* Mtn.	Top	*Map Sht. Nos.* O.S.	Bart.	*Map Reference*
	AONACH EAGACH						
39.	Sgorr nam Fiannaidh	967	183	323	41	47/50	141583
40.	Stob Coire Leith	940	—	416	41	47/50	149585
41.	Meall Dearg	953	208	376	41	47/50	161584
42.	Am Bodach	943	—	404	41	47/50	168580
	APPIN						
43.	Sgor na h-Ulaidh	994	146	245	41	47	111518
44.	Stob an Fhuarain*	968	—	322	41	47	118523
45.	Beinn Fhionnlaidh	959	196	353	50	47	095498
46.	Beinn Sgulaird	937	233	427	50	47	053461
	Beinn a' Bheithir:						
47.	Sgorr Dhonuill	1001	132	221	41	47/50	040555
48.	Sgorr Dhearg	1024	104	174	41	47/50	056558
49.	Sgorr Bhan**	947	—	389	41	47/50	063560

*Bidean nam Bian. The highest point is not shown on the O.S. 1:50,000 map.

**Not named on any map but both O.S. and Barts. show Beinn Bhan about a mile to the north of Sgor Bhan.

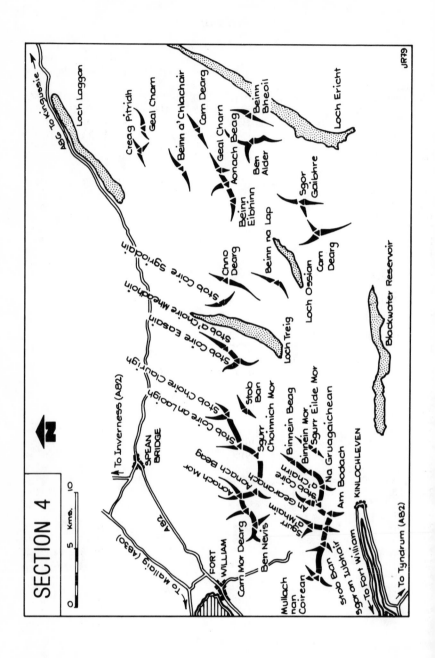

SECTION 4

Kms.

To Inverness (A82)

SPEAN BRIDGE

To Mallaig (A830)

A82

FORT WILLIAM

Carn Mor Dearg

Ben Nevis

Mullach nan Coirean

Stob Ban

Sgor an Iubhair

Aonach Mor

Aonach Beag

Sgurr a'Mhaim

An Gearanach

Stob Coire a' Chairn

Binnein Beag

Binnein Mor

Sgurr Eilde Mor

Na Gruagaichean

Am Bodach

KINLOCHLEVEN

To Fort William

To Tyndrum (A82)

Sgurr Choinnich Mor

Stob Ban

Stob Coire an Laoigh

Stob Choire Claurigh

Stob Coire Easain

Stob a'Choire Mheadhoin

Stob Coire Sgriodain

Chno Dearg

Beinn na Lap

Loch Treig

Loch Ossian

Carn Dearg

Blackwater Reservoir

A86 To Kingussie

Loch Laggan

Creag Pitridh

Geal Charn

Beinn a'Chlachair

Carn Dearg

Geal Charn

Aonach Beag

Beinn Eibhinn

Ben Alder

Sgor Gaibhre

Loch Ericht

Beinn Bheoil

JR79

Table I. Arranged according to Districts 21

SECTION 4

	NAME	Height	No. in order of Altitude		Map Sht. Nos.		Map
			Mtn.	Top	O.S.	Bart.	Reference
	THE MAMORES						
1.	Sgurr Eilde Mor............	1008	120	203	41	48/50/51	231658
2.	Binnein Beag	940	228	413	41	50/51	222677
3.	Binnein Mor...............	1128	30	47	41	48/50/51	212663
4.	Binnein Mor—South Top...	1059	—	120	41	48/50/51	211657
5.	Sgurr Eilde Beag*	956	—	364	41	48/50/51	219653
6.	Na Gruagaichean............	1055	71	122	41	48/50/51	203652
	Na Gruagaichean—						
7.	North-west Top	1036c	—	158	41	48/50/51	201654
8.	An Gearanach*	982†	162	274	41	48/50/51	187670
9.	An Garbhanach...........	975	—	303	41	48/50/51	188665
10.	Stob Coire a' Chairn*........	981	165	277	41	48/50/51	185661
11.	Am Bodach	1032	96	162	41	48/50/51	176651
12.	Sgor an Iubhair*	1001	133	222	41	48/50/51	165655
13.	Stob Choire a' Mhail*......	980c	—	283	41	48/50/51	163659
14.	Sgurr a' Mhaim	1099	49	81	41	48/50/51	165667
15.	Stob Ban...................	999	138	232	41	48/50/51	148654
16.	Mullach nan Coirean	939	231	420	41	50	122662
	Mullach nan Coirean—						
17.	South-east Top	917	—	509	41	50	131655
	BEN NEVIS and THE AONACHS						
18.	Ben Nevis	1344	1	1	41	50/51	166713
	Carn Dearg—						
19.	South-west Top	1020	—	182	41	50/51	155701
	Carn Dearg—						
20.	North-west Top	1221	—	12	41	50/51	159719
21.	Carn Mor Dearg	1223	7	10	41	50/51	177722
22.	Carn Dearg Meadhonach ...	1179†	—	21	41	50/51	176727
23.	Aonach Mor................	1221†	8	11	41	50/51	193730
24.	Stob an Cul Choire**	1097c	—	83	41	50/51	203732
25.	Tom na Sroine**..........	918	—	499	41	50/51	208745
26.	Aonach Beag	1234†	6	9	41	50/51	196715
27.	Stob Coire Bhealaich	1101†	—	78	41	50/51	202709
28.	Sgurr a' Bhuic	965	—	332	41	50/51	204702
	GREY CORRIES						
29.	Sgurr Choinnich Mor	1095	50	84	41	50/51	227714
30.	Sgurr Choinnich Beag......	966	—	327	41	50/51	220710
31.	Stob Coire an Laoigh*	1115	37	59	41	50/51	240725
32.	Stob Coire Easain	1080	—	99	41	50/51	234727
33.	Caisteil*	1104	—	75	41	50/51	246729
34.	Beinn na Socaich	1007	—	207	41	50/51	236734
35.	Stob Coire Cath na Sine* ...	1080	—	100	41	50/51	252731
36.	Stob Choire Claurigh	1177	14	23	41	50/51	262739
37.	Stob a' Choire Leith*	1105c	—	73	41	50/51	256736

**Not named on any map.

SECTION 4 *(continued)*

	NAME	Height	No. in order of Altitude Mtn.	No. in order of Altitude Top	Map Sht. Nos. O.S.	Map Sht. Nos. Bart.	Map Reference
38.	Stob Coire na Gaibhre	955†	—	367	41	50/51	260757
39.	Stob Coire na Ceannain	1121	—	50	41	50/51	268746
40.	Stob Ban....................	977	173	293	41	50/51	266724
41.	Stob Coire Easain	1116	36	58	41	51	308730
42.	Stob a' Choire Mheadhoin....	1106	44	71	41	51	316736
	LOCH TREIG and LOCH OSSIAN						
43.	Stob Coire Sgriodain.........	976	174	296	41	51	356744
	Stob Coire Sgriodain—						
44.	South Top	960	—	351	41	51	359739
45.	Chno Dearg	1047	82	139	41	51	377741
46.	Meall Garbh..............	977	—	295	41	51	372727
47.	Beinn na Lap	937	232	426	41	51	376696
48.	Carn Dearg.................	941	225	409	42	51	418661
49.	Sgor Gaibhre	955	203	366	42	51	444674
50.	Sgor Choinnich	929	—	452	42	51	443683
	LOCH ERICHT to LOCH LAGGAN						
51.	Beinn Eibhinn	1100[1.]	47	79	42	51	449733
52.	Mullach Coire nan Nead*...	921	—	485	42	51	431734
53.	Meall Glas Choire	922c	—	480	42	51	438729
54.	Aonach Beag	1114	38	61	42	51	458742
55.	Geal-Charn*	1132	25	41	42	51	470746
56.	Sgor Iutharn*.............	1021c†	—	179	42	51	490743
57.	Carn Dearg.................	1034	95	161	42	51	504764
58.	Diollaid a' Chairn	922	—	481	42	51	488758
59.	Beinn a' Chlachair...........	1088[2.]	53	89	42	51	471781
60.	Creag Pitridh	924	260	473	42	51	488814
61.	Geal Charn[3.]	1049	78	134	42	51	504812
62.	Ben Alder..................	1148	24	38	42	51	496718
63.	Beinn Bheoil................	1019	110	184	42	51	517717
64.	Sron Coire na h-Iolaire.....	955	—	369	42	51	513704

1. Beinn Eibhinn. 1:25,000 map also shows 1100 at 446734.

2. Beinn a' Chlachair. Height given as 1087 in 1:25,000 map but 1:50,000 is of later date.

3. Geal Charn. Also known as Mullach Coire an Iubhair.

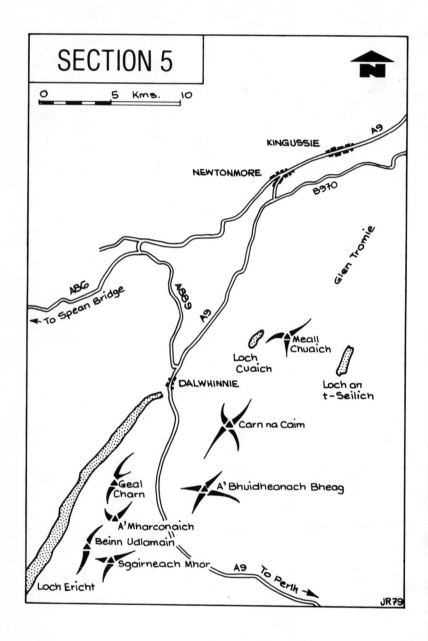

Table I. Arranged according to Districts   25

SECTION 5

	NAME	Height	No. in order of Altitude		Map Sht. Nos.		Map Reference
			Mtn.	Top	O.S.	Bart.	
	THE DRUMOCHTER HILLS						
1.	Sgairneach Mhor............	991	151	254	42	51	599731
2.	Beinn Udlamain..............	1010	119	200	42	51	579739
3.	A' Mharconaich	975	178	302	42	51	604763
4.	Geal Charn..................	917	272	506	42	51	598783
5.	Meall Chuaich	951	209	380	42	51	716879
6.	Carn na Caim...............	941	226	410	42	51	677822
7.	A' Bhuidheanach Bheag......	936	235	431	42	51	661776
8.	Glas Mheall Mor	928	—	460	42	51	681769

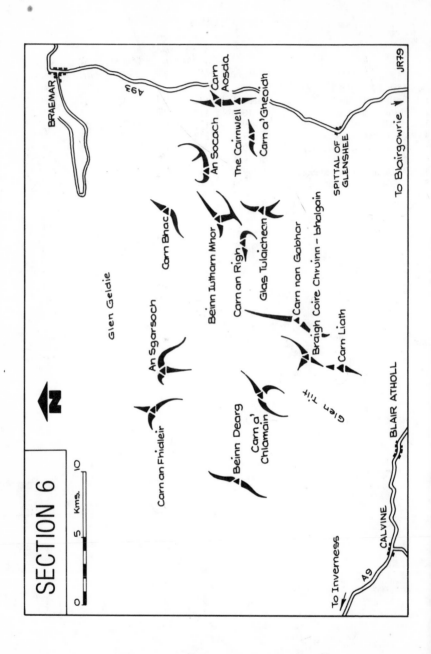

SECTION 6

To Inverness
A9
CALVINE
BLAIR ATHOLL
To Blairgowrie

SPITTAL OF GLENSHEE

BRAEMAR
A93

Glen Geldie

Glen Tilt

Carn an Fhidleir
An Sgarsoch
Carn Bhac
An Socach
Carn Aosda
The Cairnwell
Carn a'Gheoidh
Beinn Iutharn Mhor
Carn an Righ
Glas Tulaichean
Carn nan Gabhar
Braigh Coire Chruinn - bhalgain
Carn Liath
Beinn Dearg
Carn a' Chlamain

0   5   Kms.   10

N

JR79

Table I. Arranged according to Districts 27

SECTION 6

	NAME	Height	No. in order of Altitude Mtn.	No. in order of Altitude Top	Map Sht. Nos. O.S.	Map Sht. Nos. Bart.	Map Reference
	THE TARF and TILT HILLS						
1.	Carn an Fhidhleir (Carn Ealar)	994	145	244	43	51	905842
2.	An Sgarsoch...............	1006	124	209	43	51	933836
3.	Beinn Dearg...............	1008	121	204	43	51	853778
4.	Carn a' Chlamain	963	188	334	43	51	916758
	Beinn a' Ghlo:—						
5.	Carn nan Gabhar............	1129	29	46	43	51	971733
6.	Airgiod Bheinn	1061	—	118	43	51	962720
7.	Braigh Coire Chruinn-bhalgain	1070c†	63	107	43	51	946724
8.	Carn Liath	975	175	299	43	51	936698
	WEST of the CAIRNWELL PASS						
9.	Glas Tulaichean............	1051	77	130	43	51/52	051760
10.	Carn an Righ	1029	98	165	43	51/52	028772
11.	Beinn Iutharn Mhor	1045	85	144	43	51/52	045792
12.	Mam nan Carn...........	986	—	266	43	51/52	049779
13.	Beinn Iutharn Bheag.......	953	—	377	43	51/52	065791
14.	Carn Bhac	946	216	391	43	51/52	051832
15.	Carn Bhac—South West Top	920	—	489	43	51/52	041827
16.	An Socach—West Summit....	944	221	399	43	51/52	079799
17.	An Socach—East Top......	938	—	422	43	51/52	099806
18.	Carn a' Gheoidh	975	177	301	43	51/52	107767
19.	Carn Bhinnein	917	—	507	43	51/52	091762
20.	The Cairnwell	933	242	439	43	51/52	135773
21.	Carn Aosda	917	270	504	43	51/52	134792

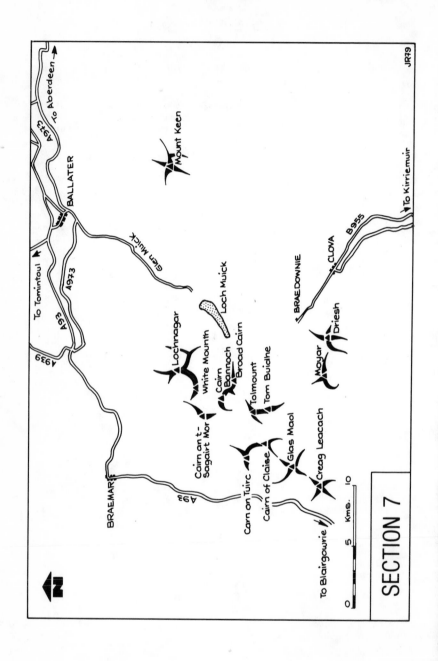

SECTION 7

Table I. Arranged according to Districts 29

SECTION 7

	NAME	Height	No. in order of Altitude Mtn.	Top	Map Sht. Nos. O.S.	Bart.	Map Reference
	GLAS MAOL HILLS						
1.	Glas Maol.................	1068	67	112	43	52	166765
2.	Meall Odhar.............	922	—	482	43	51/52	156773
3.	Little Glas Maol..........	973	—	311	43	52	175758
4.	Creag Leacach.............	987	157	263	43	51/52	155745
	Creag Leacach—						
5.	South-west Top.........	943	—	405	43	51/52	149741
6.	Cairn of Claise.............	1064	68	116	43	52	185789
7.	Druim Mor..............	961	—	341	43	52	190771
8.	Carn an Tuirc..............	1019	112	186	43	52	174804
	GLEN DOLL HILLS						
9.	Tom Buidhe...............	957	200	360	44	52	214788
10.	Tolmount.................	958	199	357	44	52	210800
11.	Crow Craigies	920	—	492	44	52	222798
12.	Cairn Bannoch.............	1012	114	193	44	52	223825
13.	Fafernie	1000	—	228	44	52	215823
14.	Cairn of Gowal	983	—	272	44	52	227817
15.	Craig of Gowal	927	—	466	44	52	232809
16.	Broad Cairn...............	998	139	234	44	52	240815
17.	Creag an Dubh-loch	983	—	271	44	52	233823
18.	Mayar....................	928	248	453	44	52	241738
19.	Driesh...................	947	213	386	44	52	271736
	LOCHNAGAR and WHITE MOUNTH						
20.	Lochnagar-Cac Carn Beag....	1155	19	31	44	52	244861
21.	Lochnagar-Cac Carn Mor ..	1150c†	—	37	44	52	245857
22.	Meall Coire na Saobhaidhe .	974	—	309	44	52	243873
23.	Cuidhe Crom.............	1083	—	95	44	52	260849
24.	Meikle Pap...............	980	—	288	44	52	260861
	White Mounth:—						
25.	Carn a' Coire Boidheach	1118	33	53	44	52	226845
26.	Creag a' Ghlas-uillt	1068	—	113	44	52	242842
27.	Top of Eagle's Rock	1051	—	132	44	52	237838
28.	Carn an t-Sagairt Beag	1044	—	148	44	52	216848
29.	Carn an t-Sagairt Mor........	1047	81	138	44	52	208843
30.	Mount Keen................	939	229	418	44	52	409869

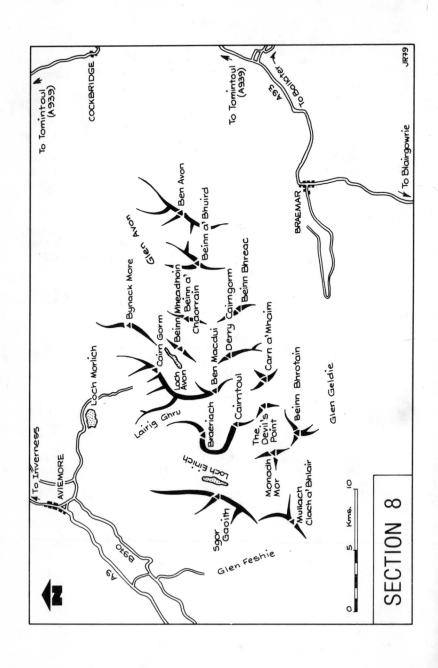

SECTION 8

Table I. Arranged according to Districts 31

SECTION 8

	NAME	Height	No. in order of Altitude Mtn.	Top	Map Sht. Nos. O.S.	Bart.	Map Reference
	GLEN FESHIE HILLS						
1.	Mullach Clach a' Bhlair	1019	111	185	35/36/43	51	883927
2.	Sgor Gaoith	1118	34	54	36/43	51	903989
3.	Meall Dubhag	998	—	237	35/36/43	51	881956
4.	Carn Ban Mor	1052	—	129	35/36/43	51	893972
5.	Sgoran Dubh Mor	1111	—	64	36	51	905002
6.	Meall Buidhe*	976	—	297	35/36	51	891001
7.	Geal Charn..............	920	—	490	35/36	51	884014
	WESTERN CAIRNGORMS						
8.	Braeriach	1296	3	3	36/43	51	953999
9.	Sron na Lairige	1184	—	17	36	51	964006
10.	Carn na Criche**.........	1265	—	6	36/43	51	939983
11.	Tom Dubh	918	—	502	36/43	51	921952
12.	Cairn Toul	1293†	4	5	36/43	51	963972
13.	Stob Coire an t-Saighdeir ...	1213	—	15	36/43	51	962963
14.	Sgor an Lochain Uaine (The Angels' Peak)	1258	—	7	36/43	51	954976
15.	The Devil's Point...........	1004	127	213	36/43	51	976951
16.	Monadh Mor	1113	39	62	43	51	938942
17.	Beinn Bhrotain	1157	18	30	43	51	954923
18.	Carn Cloich-mhuilinn......	942	—	408	43	51	968907
	MACDUI—CAIRNGORM						
19.	Carn a' Mhaim	1037	93	157	36/43	51/52	994952
20.	Ben Macdui	1309	2	2	36/43	51/52	989989
21.	Ben Macdui—North Top ...	1295	—	4	36/43	51/52	991995
22.	Sron Riach	1110c	—	67	36/43	51/52	999978
23.	Carn Etchachan..........	1120	—	52	36	51/52	003009
24.	Cairn Gorm	1245	5	8	36	51/52	005040
25.	Creag an Leth-choin (Lurcher's Crag)	1053	—	127	36	51/52	968033
26.	Cairn Lochan.............	1215	—	13	36	51/52	985025
27.	Stob Coire an t-Sneachda ...	1176	—	24	36	51/52	996029
28.	Cnap Coire na Spreidhe	1151	—	34	36	51/52	013049
	LAIRIG an LAOIGH HILLS						
29.	Bynack More	1090	52	87	36	51/52	042063
30.	Bynack Beg	964	—	333	36	51/52	035068
31.	A' Choinneach............	1017	—	187	36	51/52	032048
32.	Beinn Mheadhoin	1182	12	19	36	51/52	024016
33.	Beinn Mheadhoin—South-west Top	1163	—	29	36	51/52	018011
34.	Stob Coire Etchachan......	1082	—	97	36	51/52	024005
35.	Stacan Dubha	1013	—	192	36	51/52	012014

**Not named on any map.

	NAME	Height	No. in order of Altitude		Map Sht. Nos.		Map Reference
			Mtn.	Top	O.S.	Bart.	
36.	Derry Cairngorm............	1155	20	32	36/43	51/52	017980
37.	Sgurr an Lochan Uaine.....	983	—	273	36/43	51/52	025991
38.	Creagan a' Choire Etchachan	1108	—	69	36/43	51/52	012996
39.	Beinn Bhreac	931	245	443	43/36	51/52	058970
40.	Beinn Bhreac—West Top ...	927	—	464	43/36	51/52	052972
41.	Beinn a' Chaorainn	1082	58	96	36	51/52	045013
42.	Beinn a' Chaorainn Bheag...	1015	—	189	36	51/52	058018
	EASTERN CAIRNGORMS Ben Avon:						
43.	Leabaidh an Daimh Bhuidhe ..	1171	16	27	36	51/52	132019
44.	East Meur Gorm Craig	935	—	435	36	51/52	159042
45.	West Meur Gorm Craig*....	1021c	—	178	36	51/52	154035
46.	Carn Eas.................	1089	—	88	43/36	51/52	122992
47.	Creag an Dail Mhor........	972	—	313	43/36	51/52	132982
48.	Beinn a' Bhuird—North Top ..	1196	10	16	36	51/52	092005
49.	South Top...............	1179	—	22	43/36	51/52	093986
50.	Cnap a' Chleirich..........	1172	—	26	36	51/52	108009
51.	Stob an t-Sluichd	1106	—	72	36	51/52	112027

Stob an t-Sluichd has two tops, both 1106, about 200m apart on the 1:25,000 map.

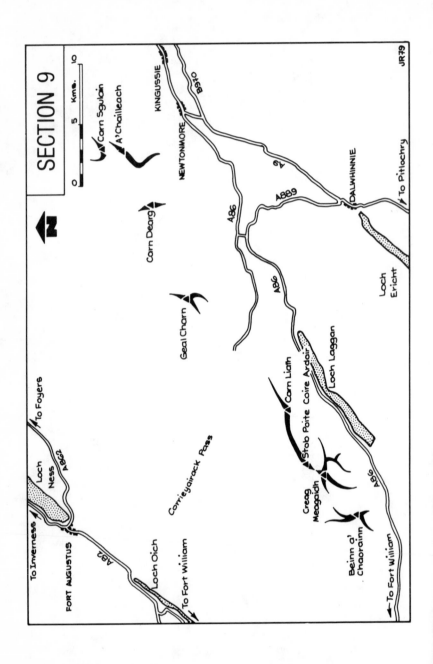

Table I. Arranged according to Districts 35

SECTION 9

	NAME	Height	No. in order of Altitude Mtn.	Top	Map Sht. Nos. O.S.	Bart.	Map Reference
	LOCH LAGGAN HILLS						
1.	Beinn a' Chaorainn..........	1052	76	128	34/41	51	386851
2.	South Top	1050	—	133	34/41	51	386845
3.	North Top	1045	—	145	34/41	51	384857
4.	Creag Meagaidh	1130	26	43	34/42	51	418875
5.	An Cearcallach	993	—	248	34/42	51	422854
6.	Meall Coire Choille-rais	1027	—	171	34/42	51	433862
7.	Puist Coire Ardair*........	1070	—	108	34/42	51	436873
8.	Sron a' Choire [+]	1001	—	225	34/42	51	448878
9.	Stob Poite Coire Ardair	1053	75	126	34/42	51	429888
10.	East Top.................	1051	—	131	34/42	51	437892
11.	Sron Coire a' Chriochairein .	991	—	255	34/42	51	447899
12.	Carn Liath	1006	123	208	34	51	472903
13.	Meall an-t-Snaim*.........	969	—	317	34	51	459905
14.	Stob Coire Dubh*	916**	—	512	34	51	496917
	THE MONADH LIATH						
15.	Geal Charn.................	926	256	468	35	51	561988
16.	Carn Dearg.................	945	219	397	35	51	635024
17.	South-east Top	923[+]	—	479	35	51	637018
18.	Carn Ban	942	—	406	35	51	632031
19.	Carn Ballach	920	—	491	35	51	643045
20.	Carn Sgulain	920	263	487	35	51	684059
21.	A' Chailleach..............	930	247	448	35	51	681041

[+] *O.S. Sheet 34 gives this as "Ghoire".*
**O.S. *only shows a contour height of 910 but the highest point is 916. Top is not named on any map. On 1:10,000 there is Coire Dubh with Allt a' Choire Dhuibh flowing down from it.*

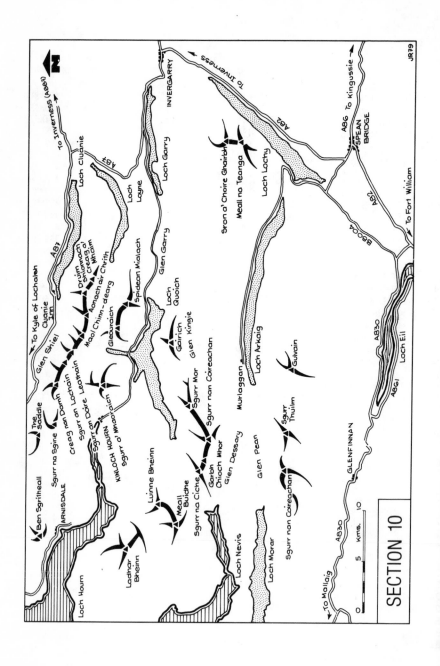

SECTION 10

Table I. Arranged according to Districts 37

North of the Great Glen

SECTION 10

	NAME	Height	No. in order of Altitude Mtn.	Top	Map Sht. Nos. O.S.	Bart.	Map Reference
	LOCH LOCHY HILLS						
1.	Meall na Teanga	917	271	505	34	50/51	220925
2.	Sron a' Choire Ghairbh	935	237	433	34	50/51	222945
	GULVAIN and GLEN PEAN						
3.	Gaor Bheinn (or Gulvain).	987	156	262	41	50	002876
4.	South Top	962†	—	338	40	50	997864
5.	Sgurr Thuilm	963	189	335	40	50	939879
6.	Sgurr nan Coireachan	956	202	362	40	50	903880
	CICHE—KINGIE						
7.	Sgurr na Ciche	1040	89	152	33/40	50	902966
8.	Garbh Chioch Mhor	1013	113	191	33/40	50	909961
9.	Garbh Chioch Bheag*	968	—	321	33/40	50	918959
10.	Sgurr nan Coireachan	953	207	375	33/40	50	933958
11.	Sgurr Mor.	1003	128	215	33/40	50	965980
12.	Gairich	919	265	493	33	50	025995
	KNOYDART and SGRITHEALL						
13.	Meall Buidhe	946	215	390	33/40	50	849989
14.	South-east Top	940c†	—	414	33/40	50	853987
15.	Luinne Bheinn	939	230	419	33	50	869008
16.	East Top.	937	—	428	33	50	872007
17.	Ladhar Bheinn.	1020	108	181	33	50	824040
18.	Stob a' Choire Odhair.	960c	—	347	33	50	830043
19.	Beinn Sgritheall	974	180	305	33	50/54	836126
20.	North-west Top	928	—	458	33	50/54	835131
	LOCH QUOICH						
21.	Sgurr a' Mhaoraich.	1027	101	169	33	50	984065
22.	Sgurr a' Mhaoraich Beag* . .	948	—	384	33	50	977067
23.	Gleouraich	1035	94	160	33	50	039054
24.	Craig Coire na Fiar Bhealaich	1006	—	210	33	50	047051
25.	Spidean Mialach	996	143	240	33	50	066043
	SOUTH GLEN SHIEL						
26.	Creag a' Mhaim.	947	214	387	33	50	088078
27.	Druim Shionnach	987	155	261	33	50	074085
28.	Aonach air Chrith	1021	107	177	33	50	051083
29.	Maol Chinn-dearg	981	166	278	33	50	032088
30.	Sgurr an Doire Leathain	1010	116	197	33	50	015099
31.	Sgurr an Lochain.	1004	126	212	33	50	005104
32.	Creag nan Damh	918	268	497	33	50/54	983112

SECTION 10 *(continued)*

	NAME	Height	No. in order of Altitude Mtn.	Top	Map Sht. Nos. O.S.	Bart.	Map Reference
	THE SADDLE GROUP						
33.	The Saddle	1010*	118	199	33	50	936131
34.	Trig Point................	1010	—	201	33	50	934131
35.	West Top	968c	—	318	33	50	928128
36.	Spidean Dhomhuill Bhric...	940	—	417	33	50	922129
37.	Sgurr Leac nan Each.......	919	—	494	33	50	918133
38.	East Top.................	958	—	359	33	50	938130
39.	Sgurr na Forcan**.........	960c	—	346	33	50	941131
40.	Sgurr na Sgine	945	220	398	33	50	946113
41.	North-west Top...........	944	—	401	33	50	944115

Observation on the ground gives the impression that the main summit of The Saddle is slightly higher than the Trig Point.

**Not named on any map.*

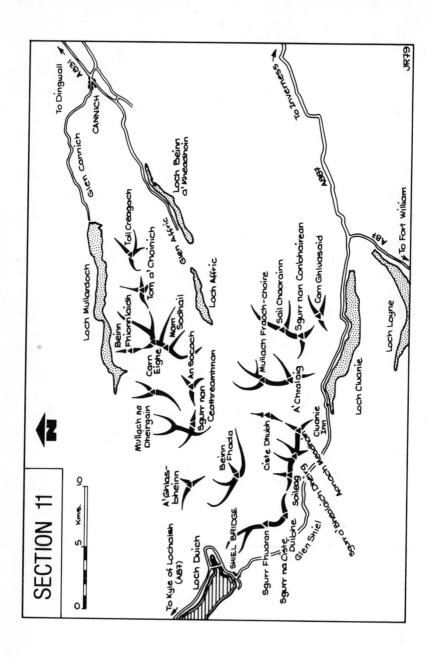

SECTION 11

N

0   5   Kms.   10

To Kyle of Lochalsh (A87)

Loch Duich

SHIEL BRIDGE

A'Ghlas-bheinn

Mullach na Dheirgain

Sgurr nan Ceathreamhnan

Carn Eighe

Mullach na Dheirgain

Beinn Fhionnlaidh

Mam Sodhail

Tom a'Choinich

Toll Creagach

Glen Cannich

Loch Mullardoch

To Dingwall

A831

CANNICH

Loch Beinn a' Mheadhoin

Glen Affric

Loch Affric

An Socach

Beinn Fhada

Sgurr Fhuaran

Sgurr na Ciste Duibhe

Saileag

Glen Shiel

Ciste Dhubh

Sgurr a' Bhealaich Dheirg

A'Chralaig

Mullach Fraoch-choire

Sail Chaorainn

Sgurr nan Conbhairean

Carn Ghluasaid

Cluanie Inn

Loch Cluanie

A887

Loch Loyne

To Inverness

A87

To Fort William

JR79

Table I. Arranged according to Districts 41

SECTION 11

	NAME	Height	No. in order of Altitude Mtn.	Top	Map Sht. Nos. O.S.	Bart.	Map Reference
	NORTH GLEN SHIEL						
	THE FIVE SISTERS to CISTE DHUBH						
1.	Sgurr Fhuaran	1068	66	111	33	54/50	978167
2.	Sgurr nan Saighead	929	—	451	33	54/50	975178
3.	Sgurr na Carnach	1002	—	219	33	54/50	977159
4.	Sgurr na Ciste Duibhe........	1027	102	170	33	54/50	984149
5.	Sgurr nan Spainteach	990c	—	256	33	54/50	992150
6.	Saileag	959	195	352	33	54/50	018148
7.	Sgurr a' Bhealaich Dheirg	1038	92	156	33	54/50	035143
8.	Aonach Meadhoin*..........	1003	129	216	33	54/50	049137
9.	Sgurr an Fhuarail	988	—	259	33	54/50	054139
10.	Ciste Dhubh................	982	163	275	33	54/50	062166
	A' CHRALAIG—CONBHAIREAN GROUP						
11.	Mullach Fraoch-choire.......	1102	46	77	33	54/50	095171
12.	A' Chralaig	1120	32	51	33	54/50	094148
13.	Stob Coire na Cralaig	1008	—	205	33	54/50	091163
14.	A' Chioch................	948	—	385	34	54/50	108153
15.	Sail Chaorainn..............	1002	131	218	34	55/50	133154
16.	Carn na Coire Mheadhoin* .	1001	—	224	34	55/50	134159
17.	Tigh Mor na Seilge	929	—	450	34	55/50	141166
18.	Sgurr nan Conbhairean	1110	42	66	34	55/50	129139
19.	Drochaid an Tuill Easaich* .	1000	—	229	34	55/50	121134
20.	Creag a' Chaorainn*.......	999	—	233	34	55/50	137131
21.	Carn Ghluasaid	957	201	361	34	50/54	146125
	GLEANN LICHD—GLEN AFFRIC						
22.	A' Ghlas-bheinn	918	269	498	25/33	54	008231
23.	Beinn Fhada (Ben Attow).....	1032	97	163	33	50/54	018192
24.	Meall an Fhuarain Mhoir* . .	956	—	363	33	50/54	000196
25.	Sgurr a' Dubh Doire*	963	—	337	33	50/54	035185
	GLEN AFFRIC						
26.	Sgurr nan Ceathreamhnan	1151	21	33	25/33	54	057228
27.	West Top*	1143	—	40	25/33	54	053228
28.	Stob Coire nan Dearcag* ...	940	—	415	25/33	54	071225
29.	Stuc Bheag	1074c†	—	104	25/33	54	053237
30.	Stuc Mor*................	1043	—	150	25/33	54	054243
31.	Mullach na Dheiragain	982	164	276	25/33	54	081259
32.	Mullach Sithidh*..........	973	—	312	25/33	54	082264
33.	Carn na Con Dhu*	968c†	—	319	25/33	54	073242
34.	An Socach**	920	264	488	25/33	54	088230
35.	Mam Sodhail	1180	13	20	25	54	120253
36.	Creag Coire nan Each	1056	—	121	25	54	113234
37.	An Tudair................	1074	—	105	25	55	127239
38.	Mullach Cadha Rainich* ...	993	—	249	25	55	139246
39.	Sgurr na Lapaich..........	1036	—	159	25	55	154243

**Not named on any map

SECTION 11 *(continued)*

	NAME	Height	No. in order of Altitude Mtn.	Top	Map Sht. Nos. O.S.	Bart.	Map Reference
40.	Carn Eighe	1183	11	18	25	54	123262
41.	Stob Coire Lochan	917	—	508	25	54	119272
42.	Stob a' Choire Dhomhain . .	1148	—	39	25	54	133265
43.	Sron Garbh*	1132	—	42	25	55	145264
44.	Beinn Fhionnlaidh.	1005	125	211	25	54	115282
45.	Tom a' Choinich	1111	40	63	25	55	163273
46.	Tom a' Choinich Beag*	1029	—	167	25	55	157273
47.	An Leth-chreag*	1044c	—	146	25	55	153269
48.	Toll Creagach	1054	73	124	25	55	194283
49.	Toll Creagach—West Top . .	952	—	378	25	55	177275

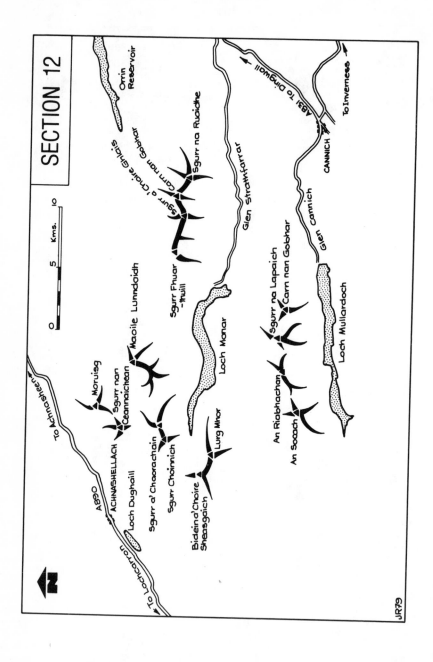

SECTION 12

Orrin Reservoir

To Achnasheen

A890

ACHNASHELLACH

Loch Dughaill

To Lochcarron

Moruisg

Sgurr nan Ceannaichean

Maoile Lunndaidh

Sgurr a' Chaorachain

Sgurr Choinnich

Bideina'Choire Sheasgaich

Lurg Mhor

Sgurr a' Choire Ghlais

Carn nan Gobhar

Sgurr na Ruaidhe

Sgurr Fhuar-thuill

Glen Strathfarrar

Loch Monar

An Riabhachan

An Socach

Sgurr na Lapaich

Carn nan Gobhar

Glen Cannich

Loch Mullardoch

A831 To Dingwall

CANNICH

To Inverness

0   5   Kms.   10

JR79

Table I. Arranged according to Districts 45

SECTION 12

	NAME	Height	No. in order of Altitude Mtn.	Top	Map Sht. Nos. O.S.	Bart.	Map Reference
	SGURR NA LAPAICH GROUP						
1.	Carn nan Gobhar	992	149	250	25	55	182344
2.	Creag Dubh	946	—	394	25	55	200351
3.	Sgurr na Lapaich...........	1150	22	35	25	55	161351
4.	Sgurr nan Clachan Geala* ..	1095	—	85	25	55	162342
5.	An Riabhachan	1129	28	45	25	54/55	134345
6.	North-east Top	1117c	—	57	25	54/55	139348
7.	South-west Top	1086	—	91	25	54	123336
8.	West Top	1040	—	153	25	54	117338
9.	An Socach*	1069	64	109	25	54	100332
	THE STRATHFARRAR HILLS						
10.	Sgurr na Ruaidhe...........	993	148	247	25	55	289425
11.	Carn nan Gobhar	992	150	251	25	55	273439
12.	Sgurr a' Choire Ghlais	1083	56	93	25	55	259430
13.	Sgurr Fhuar-thuill...........	1049	79	135	25	55	236437
14.	Creag Ghorm a' Bhealaich..	1030	—	164	25	55	244435
15.	Sgurr na Fearstaig	1015	—	190	25	55	228437
	EAST of ACHNASHELLACH						
16.	Moruisg	928	252	457	25	54	101499
17.	Sgurr nan Ceannaichean......	915	275	514	25	54	087480
18.	Maoile Lunndaidh...........	1007	122	206	25	55/54	135458
19.	Carn nam Fiaclan	996	—	242	25	54	123454
20.	Sgurr a' Chaorachain	1053	74	125	25	54	087447
21.	Bidean an Eoin Deirg	1046	—	143	25	54	103443
22.	Sgurr Choinnich	999	136	230	25	54	076446
23.	Bidein a' Choire Sheasgaich...	945	218	396	25	54	049412
24.	Lurg Mhor	986	158	264	25	54	065404
25.	Meall Mor	974	—	308	25	54	072405

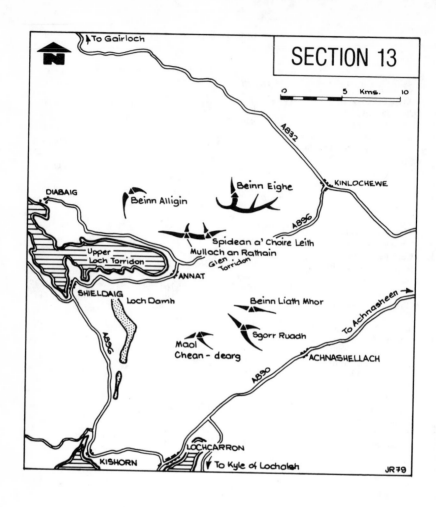

Table I. Arranged according to Districts 47

SECTION 13

	NAME	Height	No. in order of Altitude Mtn.	Top	Map Sht. Nos. O.S.	Bart.	Map Reference
	STRATH CARRON—GLEN TORRIDON						
1.	Maol Chean-dearg...........	933	241	438	25	54	924498
2.	Sgorr Ruadh................	960c	191	343	25	54	959504
3.	Beinn Liath Mhor	925	258	470	25	54	964519
	THE TORRIDONS						
4.	Beinn Alligin—Sgurr Mhor ...	985	160	267	19/24	54	866613
5.	Tom na Gruagaich	922	—	484	19/24	54	859601
	Liathach—						
6.	Spidean a' Choire Leith	1054	72	123	25	54	929579
7.	Mullach an Rathain..........	1023	105	175	25	54	912577
8.	Northern Pinnacles*.......	953c	—	374	25	54	914579
9.	Am Fasarinen	927	—	463	25	54	924575
10.	Stob a' Coire Liath Mhor ...	983c	—	270	25	54	933581
	Beinn Eighe—						
11.	Ruadh-stac-Mor	1010	117	198	19	54	951611
12.	Sail Mhor	981	—	280	19	54	938605
13.	Coinneach Mhor*	975c	—	298	19	54	944600
14.	Spidean Coire nan Clach* ..	972	—	314	25	54	965597
15.	Sgurr Ban................	971	—	315	25	54	974600
16.	Sgurr nan Fhir Duibhe*	963	—	336	25	54	982600

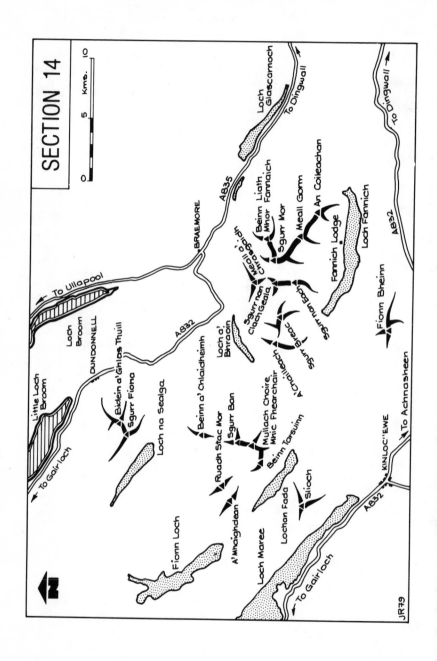

Table I. Arranged according to Districts 49

SECTION 14

	NAME	Height	No. in order of Altitude Mtn.	Top	Map Sht. Nos. O.S.	Bart.	Map Reference
	SLIOCH—AN TEALLACH GROUP						
1.	Slioch—Trig Point	980	169	285	19	54	005688
2.	North Top	980	—	287	19	54	004691
3.	Sgurr an Tuill Bhain	933	—	441	19	54	018689
4.	Ruadh Stac Mor	918	267	496	19	58	018756
5.	A' Mhaighdean	967†	184	324	19	54/58	007748
6.	Beinn Tarsuinn	936†	234	430	19	54	039727
7.	Mullach Coire Mhic Fhearchair	1019	109	183	19	54/58	052735
8.	East Top.................	981	—	282	19	54/58	056734
9.	Sgurr Dubh	918	—	501	19	54/58	061729
10.	Sgurr Ban..................	989	153	258	19	54/58	055745
11.	Beinn a' Chlaidheimh	914	276	516	19	58	061775
	An Teallach—						
12.	Bidein a' Ghlas Thuill........	1062	69	117	19	58	069843
13.	Glas Mheall Mor	981	—	281	19	58	076854
14.	Glas Mheall Liath	962†	—	339	19	58	077841
15.	Sgurr Fiona	1059	70	119	19	58	064837
16.	Sgurr Creag an Eich	1016†	—	188	19	58	055838
17.	Lord Berkeley's Seat	1047c	—	137	19	58	064834
18.	Corrag Bhuidhe...........	1020c	—	180	19	58	065833
19.	Corrag Bhuidhe Buttress* ..	945c†	—	395	19	58	066831
20.	Stob Cadha Gobhlach......	960†	—	345	19	58	068825
21.	Sail Liath	954	—	373	19	58	071824
	THE FANNAICHS						
22.	A' Chailleach..............	999	137	231	19	54	136714
23.	Toman Coinich*	937	—	425	20	54	148714
24.	Sgurr Breac	1000	135	227	20	54/55	158711
25.	Meall a' Chrasgaidh	934	239	436	20	55	184733
26.	Sgurr nan Clach Geala	1093	51	86	20	55	184715
27.	Sgurr nan Each	923	262	478	20	55	184697
28.	Sgurr Mor.................	1110	41	65	20	55	203718
29.	Carn na Criche............	961	—	342	20	55	196725
30.	Meall nam Peithirean*	974	—	306	20	55	207708
31.	Beinn Liath Mhor Fannaich...	954	204	370	20	55	219724
32.	Meall Gorm	949	210	381	20	55	221696
33.	South-east Top	922	—	483	20	55	232692
34.	An Coileachan.............	923	261	477	20	55	241680
35.	Fionn Bheinn	933	240	437	20	55	147621

† Outdoor Leisure map.

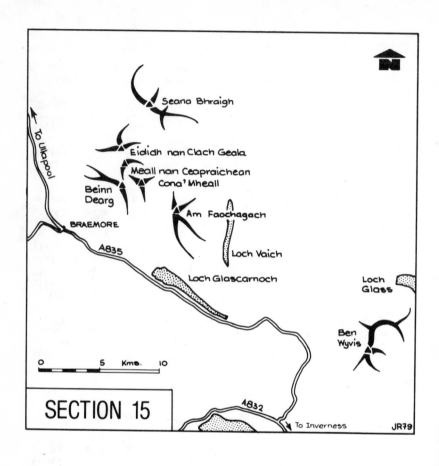

SECTION 15

Table I. Arranged according to Districts   51

SECTION 15

	NAME	Height	No. in order of Altitude Mtn.	Top	Map Sht. Nos. O.S.	Bart.	Map Reference
	BEN WYVIS and the BEINN DEARG GROUP						
	Ben Wyvis—						
1.	Glas Leathad Mor	1046	83	141	20	59	463684
2.	An Cabar	946†	—	393	20	59	450665
3.	Tom a' Choinnich	955	—	368	20	59	463700
4.	Glas Leathad Beag*	928	—	459	20	59	492706
5.	Am Faochagach.	954	206	372	20	58	303793
6.	Cona' Mheall	980	170	286	20	58	274816
7.	Beinn Dearg	1084	55	92	20	58	259812
8.	Meall nan Ceapraichean	977	172	292	20	58	257825
9.	Ceann Garbh*	967	—	325	20	58	259831
10.	Eididh nan Clach Geala	928	249	454	20	58	257842
11.	Seana Bhraigh	927	254	462	20	58	281878

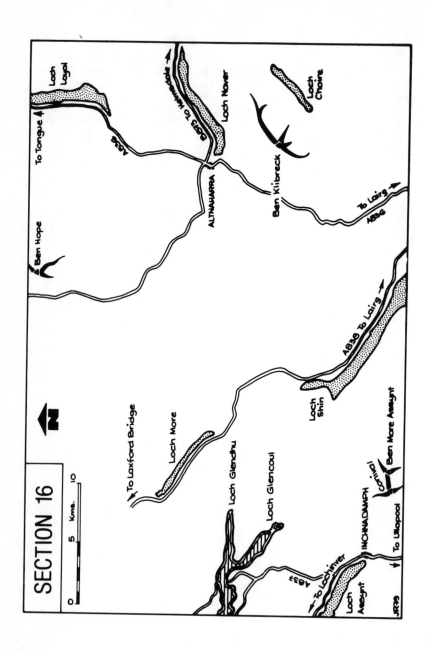

SECTION 16

Table I. Arranged according to Districts 53

SECTION 16

	NAME	Height	No. in order of Altitude		Map Sht. Nos.		Map Reference
			Mtn.	Top	O.S.	Bart.	
	ASSYNT						
1.	Ben More Assynt............	998	140	235	15	58	318201
2.	South Top	960	—	348	15	58	324193
3.	Conival....................	987	154	260	15	58	303199
	HOPE and KLIBRECK						
4.	Ben Hope..................	927	253	461	9	60	477501
5.	Ben Klibreck	961	190	340	16	60	585299

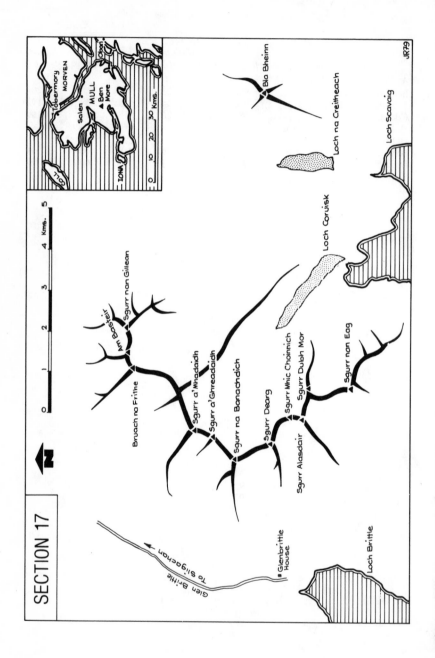

SECTION 17

Table I. Arranged according to Districts 55

SECTION 17

The Islands

	NAME	Height	No. in order of Altitude Mtn.	Top	Map Sht. Nos. O.S.	Bart.	Map Reference
	MULL						
1.	Ben More	966	185	326	48	47	526331
	SKYE						
	THE CUILLIN						
	SLIGACHAN HILLS						
2.	Sgurr nan Gillean	965	187	331	32	54	472253
3.	Am Basteir	935	236	432	32	54	465253
4.	Bhasteir Tooth............	914c	—	515	32	54	464252
5.	Bruach na Frithe	958	198	356	32	54	461252
6.	Sgurr a' Fionn Choire......	930c	—	447	32	54	463252
	THE CENTRAL CUILLIN						
7.	Sgurr a' Mhadaidh-S.W. Peak	918	266	495	32	54	446235
8.	Sgurr a' Ghreadaidh	973	181	310	32	54	445232
9.	South Top	969	—	316	32	54	445229
	GLEN BRITTLE HILLS						
10.	Sgurr na Banachdich-North Peak	965	186	330	32	54	440225
11.	Central Top	942	—	407	32	54	442222
12.	Sgurr Thormaid*..........	927	—	465	32	54	441226
	Sgurr Dearg—						
13.	Inaccessible Pinnacle	986	159	265	32	54	444215
14.	Sgurr Dearg—Cairn	978	—	291	32	54	443216
15.	Sgurr Mhic Choinnich	948	211	382	32	54	450210
16.	Sgurr Alasdair	993	147	246	32	54	449208
17.	Sgurr Thearlaich*	984	—	269	32	54	451208
18.	Sgurr Sgumain............	947	—	388	32	54	448206
	THE SOUTHERN CUILLIN						
19.	Sgurr Dubh Mor	944	222	400	32	54	457205
20.	Sgurr Dubh na Da Bheinn* .	938	—	423	32	54	455204
21.	Sgurr nan Eag	924	259	472	32	54	457195
22.	Bla Bheinn (Blaven)	928	251	456	32	54	530217
23.	South-west Top	924	—	475	32	54	528215

TABLE II

THE 3000-FEET TOPS ARRANGED IN ORDER OF ALTITUDE

No. in order of Alt.				
Mtn.	*Top*	*Height*	*Name*	*Sect.Ref. Table I*
1	1	1344	Ben Nevis	4-18
2	2	1309	Ben Macdui	8-20
3	3	1296	Braeriach	8- 8
–	4	1295	Ben Macdui—North Top	8-21
4	5	1293†	Cairn Toul	8-12
–	6	1265	Carn na Criche......................	8-10
–	7	1258	Sgor an Lochain Uaine	8-14
5	8	1245	Cairn Gorm	8-24
6	9	1234†	Aonach Beag	4-26
7	10	1223	Carn Mor Dearg	4-21
8	11	1221†	Aonach Mor.........................	4-23
–	12	1221†	Carn Dearg-North-west Top	4-20
–	13	1215	Cairn Lochan.......................	8-26
9	14	1214	Ben Lawers..........................	2-12
–	15	1213	Stob Coire an t-Saighdeir	8-13
10	16	1196	Beinn a' Bhuird—North Top	8-48
–	17	1184	Sron na Lairige	8- 9
11	18	1183	Carn Eighe..........................	11-40
12	19	1182	Beinn Mheadhoin	8-32
13	20	1180	Mam Sodhail	11-35
–	21	1179†	Carn Dearg Meadhonach	4-22
–	22	1179	Beinn a' Bhuird—South Top	8-49
14	23	1177	Stob Choire Claurigh	4-36
–	24	1176	Stob Coire an t-Sneachda............	8-27
15	25	1174	Ben More (Crianlarich)...............	1-20
–	26	1172	Cnap a' Chleirich	8-50
16	27	1171	Ben Avon—Leabaidh an Daimh Bhuidhe	8-43
17	28	1165	Stob Binnein	1-21
–	29	1163	Beinn Mheadhoin—South-west Top...	8-33
18	30	1157	Beinn Bhrotain	8-17
19	31	1155	Lochnagar—Cac Carn Beag	7-20
20	32	1155	Derry Cairngorm.....................	8-36
21	33	1151	Sgurr nan Ceathreamhnan.............	11-26
–	34	1151	Cnap Coire na Spreidhe	8-28
22	35	1150	Sgurr na Lapaich	12- 3
23	36	1150	Bidean nam Bian	3-33
–	37	1150c†	Lochnagar—Cac Carn Mor	7-21
24	38	1148	Ben Alder...........................	4-62
–	39	1148	Stob a' Choire Dhomhain	11-42
–	40	1143	Sgurr nan Ceathreamhnan—West Top.	11-27
25	41	1132	Geal-Charn	4-55
–	42	1132	Sron Garbh	11-43
26	43	1130	Creag Meagaidh	9- 4
27	44	1130	Ben Lui.............................	1- 9
28	45	1129	An Riabhachan	12- 5

Table II. Arranged in Order of Altitude 57

No. in order of Alt.				
Mtn.	Top	Height	Name	Sect. Ref. Table I
29	46	1129	Beinn a' Ghlo—Carn nan Gabhar.......	6- 5
30	47	1128	Binnein Mor........................	4- 3
–	48	1127	Ben Lui—North-west Top	1-10
31	49	1126	Ben Cruachan	3- 1
–	50	1121	Stob Coire na Ceannain	4-39
32	51	1120	A' Chralaig	11-12
–	52	1120	Carn Etchachan....................	8-23
33	53	1118	White Mounth—Carn a' Coire Boidheach	7-25
34	54	1118	Sgor Gaoith	8- 2
35	55	1118	Meall Garbh........................	2-15
–	56	1118	An Stuc............................	2-14
–	57	1117c	An Riabhachan—North-east Top	12- 6
36	58	1116	Stob Coire Easain	4-41
37	59	1115	Stob Coire an Laoigh	4-31
–	60	1115	Stob Coire nan Lochan..............	3-35
38	61	1114	Aonach Beag (Alder District)..........	4-54
39	62	1113	Monadh Mor	8-16
40	63	1111	Tom a' Choinich	11-45
–	64	1111	Sgoran Dubh Mor	8-5
41	65	1110	Sgurr Mor.........................	14-28
42	66	1110	Sgurr nan Conbhairean	11-18
–	67	1110c	Sron Riach	8-22
43	68	1108	Meall a' Bhuiridh	3-26
–	69	1108	Creagan a' Choire Etchachan	8-38
–	70	1107	Stob Coire nam Beith	3-34
44	71	1106	Stob a' Choire Mheadhoin............	4-42
–	72	1106	Stob an t'Sluichd..................	8-51
–	73	1105c	Stob a' Choire Leith	4-37
–	74	1104†	Stob Dearg (Taynuilt Peak)	3- 2
–	75	1104	Caisteil	4-33
45	76	1103	Bheinn Ghlas	2-17
46	77	1102	Mullach Fraoch-choire...............	11-11
–	78	1101	Stob Choire Bhealach	4-27
47	79	1100	Beinn Eibhin	4-51
48	80	1100	Creise	3-23
49	81	1099	Sgurr a' Mhaim.....................	4-14
–	82	1098	Clach Leathad	3-24
–	83	1097c	Stob an Cul Choire	4-24
50	84	1095	Sgurr Choinnich Mor	4-29
–	85	1095	Sgurr nan Clachan Geala	12- 4
51	86	1093	Sgurr nan Clach Geala	14-26
52	87	1090	Bynack More	8-29
–	88	1089	Carn Eas..........................	8-46
53	89	1088	Beinn a' Chlachair...................	4-59
54	90	1087	Stob Ghabhar	3-17
–	91	1086	An Riabhachan—South-west Top.....	12- 7
55	92	1084	Beinn Dearg........................	15- 7
56	93	1083	Sgurr a' Choire Ghlais	12-12
57	94	1083	Schiehallion	2- 1

No. in order of Alt.				Sect.Ref.
Mtn.	*Top*	*Height*	*Name*	*Table I*
–	95	1083	Cuidhe Crom	7-23
58	96	1082	Beinn a' Chaorainn	8-41
–	97	1082	Stob Coire Etchachan	8-34
59	98	1081	Beinn a' Chreachain	2-38
–	99	1080	Stob Coire Easain	4-32
–	100	1080	Stob Coire Cath na Sine	4-35
60	101	1078	Ben Starav	3-11
61	102	1076	Beinn Heasgarnich	2-25
62	103	1076†	Beinn Dorain	2-34
–	104	1074c†	Stuc Bheag	11-29
–	105	1074	An Tudair	11-37
–	106	1072	Stob Coire Sgreamhach	3-36
63	107	1070c†	Braigh Coire Chruinn-bhalgain	6- 7
–	108	1070	Puist Coire Ardair	9- 7
64	109	1069	An Socach	12- 9
65	110	1069	Meall Corranaich	2-18
66	111	1068	Sgurr Fhuaran	11- 1
67	112	1068	Glas Maol	7- 1
–	113	1068	Creag a' Ghlas-uillt	7-26
–	114	1068	Stob Coire an Lochain	1-22
–	115	1068	Stob Coire Dheirg	3-13
68	116	1064	Cairn of Claise	7- 6
69	117	1062	An Teallach—Bidein a' Ghlas Thuill	14-12
–	118	1061	Beinn a' Ghlo—Airgiod Bheinn	6- 6
70	119	1059	An Teallach—Sgurr Fiona	14-15
–	120	1059	Binnein Mor—South Top	4- 4
–	121	1056	Creag Coire nan Each	11-36
71	122	1055	Na Gruagaichean	4- 6
72	123	1054	Liathach—Spidean a' Choire Leith	13- 6
73	124	1054	Toll Creagach	11-48
74	125	1053	Sgurr a' Chaorachain	12-20
75	126	1053	Stob Poite Coire Ardair	9- 9
–	127	1053	Creag an Leth-choin (Lurcher's Crag)	8-25
76	128	1052	Beinn a' Chaorainn	9- 1
–	129	1052	Carn Ban Mor	8- 4
77	130	1051	Glas Tulaichean	6- 9
–	131	1051	Stob Poite Coire Ardair—East Top	9-10
–	132	1051	Eagle's Rock, Top of	7-27
–	133	1050	Beinn a' Chaorain—South Top	9- 2
78	134	1049	Geal Charn	4-61
79	135	1049	Sgurr Fhuar-thuill	12-13
80	136	1048†	Creag Mhor	2-26
–	137	1047c	Lord Berkeley's Seat	14-17
81	138	1047	Carn an t-Sagairt Mor	7-29
82	139	1047	Chno Dearg	4-45
–	140	1047	Creag an Fhithich	2-13
83	141	1046	Ben Wyvis—Glas Leathad Mor	15- 1
84	142	1046	Cruach Ardrain	1-18
–	143	1046	Bidean an Eoin Deirg	12-21
85	144	1045	Beinn Iutharn Mhor	6-11

Table II. Arranged in Order of Altitude   59

No. in order of Alt. Mtn.	Top	Height	Name	Sect. Ref. Table I
–	145	1045	Beinn a' Chaorainn—North Top......	9- 3
–	146	1044c	An Leth-chreag	11-47
86	147	1044	Stob Coir' an Albannaich..............	3-15
–	148	1044	White Mounth—Carn an t-Sagairt Beag	7-28
87	149	1043	Meall nan Tarmachan.................	2-20
–	150	1043	Stuc Mor.........................	11-30
88	151	1041†	Carn Mairg........................	2- 2
89	152	1040	Sgurr na Ciche....................	10- 5
–	153	1040	An Riabhachan—West Top..........	12- 8
90	154	1039	Meall Ghaordie	2-24
91	155	1039	Beinn Achaladair..................	2-36
92	156	1038	Sgurr a' Bhealaich Dheirg	11- 7
93	157	1037	Carn a' Mhaim	8-19
–	158	1036c	Na Gruagaichean—North-west Top ...	4- 7
–	159	1036	Sgurr na Lapaich...................	11-39
94	160	1035	Gleouraich	10-23
95	161	1034	Carn Dearg........................	4-57
96	162	1032	Am Bodach	4-11
97	163	1032	Beinn Fhada (Ben Attow).............	11-23
–	164	1030	Creag Ghorm a' Bhealaich...........	12-14
98	165	1029	Carn an Righ	6-10
99	166	1029	Ben Oss............................	1-11
–	167	1029	Tom a' Choinich Beag	11-46
100	168	1028†	Carn Gorm.......................	2- 8
101	169	1027	Sgurr a' Mhaoraich...................	10-21
102	170	1027	Sgurr na Ciste Duibhe...............	11- 4
–	171	1027	Meall Coire Choille-rais	9- 6
–	172	1026	Meall Garbh.......................	2-21
103	173	1025	Ben Challum	2-28
104	174	1024	Sgorr Dearg—Beinn a' Bheithir........	3-48
105	175	1023	Liathach—Mullach an Rathain........	13- 7
106	176	1022	Buachaille Etive Mor—Stob Dearg......	3-27
107	177	1021	Aonach air Chrith	10-28
–	178	1021c	West Meur Gorm Craig	8-45
–	179	1021c†	Sgor Iutharn..................	4-56
–	180	1020c	Corrag Bhuidhe....................	14-18
108	181	1020	Ladhar Bheinn.....................	10-17
–	182	1020	Carn Dearg—South-west Top	4-19
109	183	1019	Mullach Coire Mhic Fhearchair.........	14- 7
110	184	1019	Beinn Bheoil......................	4-63
111	185	1019	Mullach Clach a' Bhlair	8- 1
112	186	1019	Carn an Tuirc.......................	7- 8
–	187	1017	A' Choinneach.....................	8-31
–	188	1016c†	Sgurr Creag an Eich	14-16
–	189	1015	Beinn a' Chaorainn Bheag	8-42
–	190	1015	Sgurr na Fearstaig...................	12-15
113	191	1013	Garbh Chioch Mhor	10- 8
–	192	1013	Stacan Dubha	8-35
114	193	1012	Cairn Bannoch.....................	7-12
–	194	1012	Meall Liath (Glen Lyon).............	2- 3

No. in order of Alt. Mtn.	Top	Height	Name	Sect.Ref. Table I
115	195	1011	Beinn Ime...........................	1- 3
–	196	1011	Stob na Doire......................	3-28
116	197	1010	Sgurr an Doire Leathain...............	10-30
117	198	1010	Beinn Eighe—Ruadh-stac Mor	13-11
118	199	1010	The Saddle	10-33
119	200	1010	Beinn Udlamain.....................	5- 2
–	201	1010	The Saddle—Trig Point	10-34
–	202	1009	Drochaid Ghlas	3- 4
120	203	1008	Sgurr Eilde Mor.....................	4- 1
121	204	1008	Beinn Dearg	6- 3
–	205	1008	Stob Coire na Cralaig	11-13
122	206	1007	Maoile Lunndaidh....................	12-18
–	207	1007	Beinn na Socaich	4-34
123	208	1006	Carn Liath	9-12
124	209	1006	An Sgarsoch........................	6- 2
–	210	1006	Gleouraich—Craig Coire na Fiar Bhealaich	10-24
125	211	1005	Beinn Fhionnlaidh...................	11-44
126	212	1004	Sgurr an Lochain....................	10-31
127	213	1004	The Devil's Point....................	8-15
–	214	1004	Meall a' Bharr	2- 4
128	215	1003	Sgurr Mor..........................	10-11
129	216	1003	Aonach Meadhoin....................	11- 8
130	217	1002	Beinn an Dothaidh	2-35
131	218	1002	Sail Chaorainn......................	11-15
–	219	1002	Sgurr na Carnach	11- 3
–	220	1002	Beinn Achaladair—South Top	2-37
132	221	1001	Beinn a' Bheithir—Sgorr Dhonuill	3-47
133	222	1001	Sgor an Iubhair	4-12
134	223	1001	Meall Greigh	2-16
–	224	1001	Carn na Coire Mheadhoin	11-16
–	225	1001	Sron a' Choire (Ghoire on map)	9- 8
–	226	1000c	Beinn nan Eachan	2-22
135	227	1000	Sgurr Breac	14-24
–	228	1000	Fafernie	7-13
–	229	1000	Drochaid an Tuill Easaich	11-19
136	230	999	Sgurr Choinnich	12-22
137	231	999	A' Chailleach.......................	14-22
138	232	999	Stob Ban...........................	4-15
–	233	999	Creag a' Chaorainn.................	11-20
139	234	998	Broad Cairn	7-16
140	235	998	Ben More Assynt....................	16- 1
141	236	998	Stob Diamh	3- 5
–	237	998	Meall Dubhag	8- 3
142	238	997	Glas Bheinn Mhor...................	3-14
–	239	997	Ben Challum—South Top	2-29
143	240	996	Spidean Mialach	10-25
–	241	996	Stob a' Ghlais Choire	3-25
–	242	996	Carn nam Fiaclan	12-19
144	243	995	An Caisteal........................	1-14

Table II. Arranged in Order of Altitude   **61**

No. in order of Alt. Mtn.	Top	Height	Name	Sect.Ref. Table I
145	244	994	Carn an Fhidhleir or Carn Ealar	6- 1
146	245	994	Sgor na h-Ulaidh	3-43
147	246	993	Sgurr Alasdair	17-17
148	247	993	Sgurr na Ruaidhe.....................	12-10
–	248	993	An Cearcallach	9- 5
–	249	993	Mullach Cadha Rainich	11-38
149	250	992	Carn nan Gobhar (Sgurr na Lapaich group).............................	12- 1
150	251	992	Carn nan Gobhar (Strathfarrar)	12-11
–	252	991c	Stob Ghabhar—Aonach Eagach	3-21
–	253	991c	Sron a' Ghearrain	3-19
151	254	991	Sgairneach Mhor......................	5- 1
–	255	991	Sron Coire a' Chriochairein..........	9-11
–	256	990c	Sgurr nan Spainteach	11- 5
152	257	989	Beinn Eunaich	3- 9
153	258	989	Sgurr Ban	14-10
–	259	988	Sgurr an Fhuarail	11- 9
154	260	987	Conival..............................	16- 3
155	261	987	Druim Shionnach	10-27
156	262	987	Gaor Bheinn or Gulvain	10- 3
157	263	987	Creag Leacach	7- 4
158	264	986	Lurg Mhor	12-24
159	265	986	Inaccessible Pinnacle of Sgurr Dearg	17-13
–	266	986	Mam nan Carn.....................	6-12
160	267	985	Beinn Alligin—Sgurr Mhor	13- 4
161	268	985	Ben Vorlich (Loch Earn)	1-24
–	269	984	Sgurr Thearlaich	17-18
–	270	983c	Stob a' Coire Liath Mhor	13-10
–	271	983	Creag an Dubh-loch	7-17
–	272	983	Cairn of Gowal	7-14
–	273	983	Sgurr an Lochan Uaine..............	8-37
162	274	982	An Gearanach	4- 8
163	275	982	Ciste Dhubh.........................	11-10
164	276	982	Mullach na Dheiragain	11-31
165	277	981	Stob Coire a' Chairn..................	4-10
166	278	981	Maol Chinn-dearg....................	10-29
167	279	981	Creag Mhor	2- 5
–	280	981	Sail Mhor	13-12
–	281	981	Glas Mheall Mor	14-13
–	282	981	Mullach Coire Mhic Fhearchair—East Top	14- 8
–	283	980c	Stob Choire a' Mhail................	4-13
168	284	980	Beinn a' Chochuill....................	3- 8
169	285	980	Slioch—Trig Point	14- 1
170	286	980	Cona' Mheall........................	15- 6
–	287	980	Slioch—North Top	14- 2
–	288	980	Meikle Pap........................	7-24
–	289	980	Stob Garbh........................	3- 6
171	290	978	Beinn Dubhchraig....................	1-12
–	291	978	Cairn of Sgurr Dearg	17-14
172	292	977	Meall nan Ceapraichean..............	15- 8

No. in order of Alt. Mtn.	Top	Height	Name	Sect. Ref. Table I
173	293	977	Stob Ban........................	4-40
–	294	977	Meall Buidhe	2-39
–	295	977	Meall Garbh......................	4-46
174	296	976	Stob Coire Sgriodain................	4-43
–	297	976	Meall Buidhe	8- 6
–	298	975c	Coinneach Mhor	13-13
175	299	975	Beinn-a'-Ghlo—Carn Liath...........	6- 8
176	300	975	Stuc a' Chroin	1-25
177	301	975	Carn a' Gheoidh	6-18
178	302	975	A' Mharconaich	5- 3
–	303	975	An Garbhanach...................	4- 9
179	304	974	Ben Lomond	1- 1
180	305	974	Beinn Sgritheall..................	10-19
–	306	974	Meall nam Peithirean	14-30
–	307	974	Sron nan Giubhas	3-20
–	308	974	Meall Mor	12-25
–	309	974	Meall Coire na Saobhaidhe	7-22
181	310	973	Sgurr a' Ghreadaidh	17- 8
–	311	973	Little Glas Maol...................	7- 3
–	312	973	Mullach Sithidh..................	11-32
–	313	972	Creag an Dail Mhor	8-47
–	314	972	Spidean Coire nan Clach	13-14
–	315	971	Sgurr Ban.......................	13-15
–	316	969	Sgurr a' Ghreadaidh—South Top.....	17- 9
–	317	969	Meall an-t-Snaim..................	9-13
–	318	968c	The Saddle—West Top..............	10-35
–	319	968c†	Carn na Con Dhu	11-33
182	320	968†	Meall Garbh......................	2- 6
–	321	968	Garbh Chioch Bheag...............	10- 9
–	322	968	Stob an Fhuarain..................	3-44
183	323	967	Aonach Eagach—Sgor nam Fiannaidh...	3-39
184	324	967[1]	A' Mhaighdean	14- 5
–	325	967	Ceann Garbh	15- 9
185	326	966	Ben More—Mull	17- 1
–	327	966	Sgurr Choinnich Beag..............	4-30
–	328	966	Sron an Isean	3- 7
–	329	966	Meall na Dige.....................	1-23
186	330	965	Sgurr na Banachdich—North Peak......	17-10
187	331	965	Sgurr nan Gillean	17- 2
–	332	965	Sgurr a' Bhuic	4-28
–	333	964	Bynack Beg	8-30
188	334	963	Carn a' Chlamain	6- 4
189	335	963	Sgurr Thuilm.....................	10- 5
–	336	963	Sgurr an Fhir Duibhe	13-16
–	337	963	Sgurr a' Dubh Doire	11-25
–	338	962†	Gaor Bheinn—South Top	10- 4
–	339	962†	Glas Mheall Liath	14-14
190	340	961	Ben Klibreck	16- 5
–	341	961	Druim Mor.......................	7- 7
–	342	961	Carn na Criche...................	14-29

1. Ben Vane from Inversnaid.

H. M. Brown

D. J. Bennet

2. The A'Chir Ridge.

3. Stob Binnein from the south, with Ben More beyond.

4.   Looking west up Glen Dochard from Loch Tulla.

H. M. Brown

5. The Clachlet group seen across Rannoch Moor.

6.   Buachaille Etive Mor.

7.   Looking east along the Aonach Eagach ridge.

D. J. Bennet

8. The Devil's Ridge in the Mamores.

D. J. Bennet

9.   The C.I.C. Hut, with Carn Dearg Buttress.

10.   The summit cliffs of Ben Nevis.

11.   The Carn Mor Dearg Arete leading towards Ben Nevis.

12. The Aonachs from Sgurr a' Mhaim.

D. J. Bennet

13. Cairn Toul from Braeriach.

14. Ben Alligin from Liathach.

H. M. Brown

15. Looking west along the ridge of Beinn Eighe to Liathach.

D. J. Bennet

16. The cliffs of Sgorr Ruadh above Loch Coire Lair.

17.   Beinn Dearg Mhor from An Teallach.

18.   An Teallach, the crest of Corrag Bhuidhe and Sgurr Fiona.

D. J. Bennet

19.   Coire Mhic Fhearchair, Beinn Eighe.

H. M. Brown

20. The Coire Lagan peaks from Sgurr Dearg.

21.   Sgurr Dearg and Sgurr na Banachdich from Sgurr Alasdair.

22.   Sgurr nan Gillean.

23.   Bla Bheinn.

24. Sgurr na Ciche and Garbh Chioch Mhor from the west.

No. in order of Alt. Mtn.	Top	Height	Name	Sect. Ref. Table I
191	343	960c	Sgorr Ruadh	13- 2
192	344	960c†	Beinn nan Aighenan	3-10
–	345	960c†	Stob Cadha Goblach	14-20
–	346	960c	Sgurr na Forcan	10-39
–	347	960c	Stob a' Choire Odhair	10-18
–	348	960†	Ben More Assynt—South Top	16- 2
193	349	960	Meall Glas	2-30
194	350	960	Stuchd an Lochain	2- 9
–	351	960	Stob Coire Sgriodain—South Top	4-44
195	352	959	Saileag	11- 6
196	353	959	Beinn Fhionnlaidh	3-45
–	354	959	Cruach Ardrain—Stob Garbh	1-19
197	355	958	Buachaille Etive Beag—Stob Dubh	3-31
198	356	958	Bruach na Frithe	17- 5
199	357	958	Tolmount	7-10
–	358	958	Stob nan Clach	2-27
–	359	958	The Saddle—East Top	10-38
200	360	957	Tom Buidhe	7- 9
201	361	957	Carn Ghluasaid	11-21
202	362	956	Sgurr nan Coireachan	10- 6
–	363	956	Meall an Fhuarain Mhoir	11-24
–	364	956	Sgurr Eilde Beag	4- 5
–	365	956†	Sgor na Broige	3-30
203	366	955	Stob Gaibhre	4-49
–	367	955†	Stob Coire na Gaibhre	4-38
–	368	955	Tom a' Choinnich	15- 3
–	369	955	Sron Coire na h-Iolaire	4-64
204	370	954	Beinn Liath Mhor Fannaich	14-31
205	371	954	Beinn Mhanach	2-40
206	372	954	Am Faochagach	15- 5
–	373	954	Sail Liath	14-21
–	374	953c	Liathach—Northern Pinnacles	13- 8
207	375	953	Sgurr nan Coireachan (Glen Dessary)	10-10
208	376	953	Meall Dearg (Aonach Eagach)	3-41
–	377	953	Beinn Iutharn Bheag	6-13
–	378	952	Toll Creagach—West Top	11-49
–	379	952	Beinn Fhada (Glencoe)	3-37
209	380	951	Meal Chuaich	5- 5
210	381	949	Meall Gorm	14-32
211	382	948	Sgurr Mhic Choinnich	17-15
212	383	948	Beinn Bhuidhe	1- 7
–	384	948	Sgurr a' Mhaoraich Beag	10-22
–	385	948	A' Chioch	11-14
213	386	947	Driesh	7-19
214	387	947	Creag a' Mhaim	10-26
–	388	947	Sgurr Sgumain	17-18
–	389	947	Sgorr Bhan	3-49
215	390	946	Meall Buidhe	10-13
216	391	946	Carn Bhac	6-14
217	392	946	Beinn Tulaichean	1-17

No. in order of Alt. Mtn.	Top	Height	Name	Sect. Ref. Table I
–	393	946	An Cabar	15- 2
–	394	946	Creag Dubh	12- 2
–	395	945c†	Corrag Bhuidhe Buttress	14-19
218	396	945	Bidein a' Choire Sheasgaich.	12-23
219	397	945	Carn Dearg.	9-16
220	398	945	Sgurr na Sgine (Saddle).	10-40
221	399	944	An Socach—West Summit	6-16
222	400	944	Sgurr Dubh Mor	17-19
–	401	944	Sgurr na Sgine—North West Top	10-41
223	402	943	Stob a' Choire Odhair.	3-22
224	403	943	Ben Vorlich (Loch Lomond)	1- 5
–	404	943	Am Bodach	3-42
–	405	. 943	Creag Leacach—South West Top	7- 5
–	406	942	Carn Ban	9-18
–	407	942	Sgurr na Banachdich—Central Top . . .	17-11
–	408	942	Carn Cloich-mhuilinn.	8-18
225	409	941	Carn Dearg (Loch Ossian)	4-48
226	410	941	Carn na Caim.	5- 6
–	411	941†	Stob Coire Altruim	3-29
227	412	940	Beinn a' Chroin	1-15
228	413	940	Binnein Beag	4- 2
–	414	940c†	Meall Buidhe—South-east Top	10-14
–	415	940	Stob Coire nan Dearcag	11-28
–	416	940	Stob Coire Leith	3-40
–	417	940	Spidean Dhomhuill Bhric	10-36
229	418	939	Mount Keen	7-30
230	419	939	Luinne Bheinn	10-15
231	420	939	Mullach nan Coirean	4-16
–	421	939	Stob a' Bhruaich Leith	3-18
–	422	938	An Socach—East Top.	6-17
–	423	938	Sgurr Dubh na Da Bheinn	17-20
–	424	938	Beinn a' Chroin—West Top.	1-16
–	425	937	Toman Coinich	14-23
232	426	937	Beinn na Lap (Loch Ossian).	4-47
233	427	937	Beinn Sgulaird	3-46
–	428	937	Luinne Bheinn—East Top	10-16
–	429	937	Beinn Cheathaich . . . .'. . .	2-31
234	430	936[1]	Beinn Tarsuinn . . . .'.	14- 6
235	431	936	A' Bhuidheanach Bheag	5- 7
236	432	935	Am Basteir	17- 3
237	433	935	Sron a' Choire Ghairbh	10- 2
238	434	935	Sgiath Chuil	2-32
–	435	935	East Meur Gorm Craig	8-44
239	436	934	Meall a' Chrasgaidh	14-25
240	437	933	Fionn Bheinn	14-35
241	438	933	Maol Chean-dearg.	13- 1
242	439	933	The Cairnwell	6-20
243	440	933	Beinn Chabhair	1-13
–	441	933	Sgurr an Tuill Bhain	14- 3
244	442	932†	Meall Buidhe	2-11

1 Outdoor Leisure Map.

Table II. Arranged in Order of Altitude   65

No. in order of Alt. Mtn.	Top	Height	Name	Sect.Ref. Table I
245	443	931	Beinn Bhreac	8-39
246	444	931	Ben Chonzie (Ben-y-Hone)	1-26
–	445	931	Ben Vorlich (Loch Lomond)— North Top	1- 6
–	446	931	Beinn Fhada—North-east Top	3-38
–	447	930c	Sgurr a' Fionn Choire...............	17- 6
247	448	930	A' Chailleach........................	9-21
–	449	930	Meall Cruidh	3-12
–	450	929	Tigh Mor na Seilge	11-17
–	451	929	Sgurr nan Saighead	11- 2
–	452	929	Sgor Choinnich (Loch Ossian)........	4-50
248	453	928	Mayar..............................	7-18
249	454	928	Eididh nan Clach Geala	15-10
250	455	928	Meall nan Eun	3-16
251	456	928	Bla Bheinn (Blaven)	17-22
252	457	928	Moruisg	12-16
–	458	928	Beinn Sgritheall—North West Top....	10-20
–	459	928	Glas Leathad Beag	15- 4
–	460	928	Glas Mheall Mor	5- 8
253	461	927	Ben Hope	16- 4
254	462	927	Seana Bhraigh	15-11
–	463	927	Am Fasarinen	13- 9
–	464	927	Beinn Bhreac—West Top............	8-40
–	465	927	Sgurr Thormaid....................	17-12
–	466	927	Craig of Gowal	7-15
255	467	926 +	Beinn Narnain	1- 2
256	468	926	Geal Charn.........................	9-15
257	469	926	Meall a' Choire Leith	2-19
258	470	925	Beinn Liath Mhor	13- 3
–	471	925	Stob Coire Raineach	3-32
259	472	924	Sgurr nan Eag	17-22
260	473	924	Creag Pitridh.......................	4-60
–	474	924	Beinn a' Chuirn.....................	2-41
–	475	924	Bla Bheinn—South-west Top........	17-24
–	476	924	An Sgorr (Glen Lyon)...............	2- 7
261	477	923	An Coileachan	14-34
262	478	923	Sgurr nan Each	14-27
–	479	923†	Carn Dearg—South-east Top	9-17
–	480	922c	Meall Glas Choire	4-53
–	481	922	Diollaid a' Chairn	4-58
–	482	922	Meall Odhar.......................	7- 2
–	483	922	Meall Gorm—South-east Top	14-33
–	484	922	Tom na Gruagaich	13- 5
–	485	921	Mullach Coire nan Nead.............	4-52
–	486	920c	Sron Chona Chorein................	2-10
263	487	920	Carn Sgulain	9-20
264	488	920	An Socach	11-34
–	489	920	Carn Bhac—South-west Top........	6-15

+ *927 on 1:10,000 map*

No. in order of Alt. Mtn.	Top	Height	Name	Sect. Ref. Table I
–	490	920	Geal Charn........................	8- 7
–	491	920	Carn Ballach	9-19
–	492	920	Crow Craigies	7-11
265	493	919	Gairich...........................	10-12
–	494	919	Sgurr Leac nan Each...............	10-37
266	495	918	Sgurr a' Mhadaidh—South-west Peak ...	17- 7
267	496	918	Ruadh Stac Mor	14- 4
268	497	918	Creag nan Damh	10-32
269	498	918	A' Ghlas-bheinn	11-22
–	499	918	Tom na Sroine	4-25
–	500	918	Meall a' Churain	2-33
–	501	918	Mullach Coire Mhic Fhearchair-Sgurr Dubh..........................	14- 9
–	502	918	Tom Dubh	8-11
–	503	918	Meall Cuanail	3- 3
270	504	917	Carn Aosda	6-21
271	505	917	Meall na Teanga	10- 1
272	506	917	Geal Charn........................	5- 4
–	507	917	Carn Bhinnein	6-19
–	508	917	Stob Coire Lochan	11-41
–	509	917	Mullach nan Coirean—South-east Top	4-17
273	510	916	Beinn a' Chleibh	1- 8
–	511	916	Creag na Caillich..................	2-23
–	512	916	Stob Coire Dubh	9-14
274	513	915	Ben Vane	1- 4
275	514	915	Sgurr nan Ceannaichean.............	12-17
–	515	914c	Bhasteir Tooth....................	17- 4
276	516	914	Beinn a' Chlaidheimh	14-11

INDEX TO TABLE I, MUNRO'S TABLES

Names in brackets indicate the locality, or the "separate mtn." to which the top belongs.

MUNROISTS

Here follows the list of those who have reported that they have completed (I) Munros, (II) Tops, (III) 3000 foot mountains in the British Isles furth of Scotland, Munros and Tops being those listed in the 1981 or earlier editions of the Tables. Future claims must be based on the 1984 Edition. Existing Munroists are advised that there are no new Munros and Tops to climb.

* denotes a member or former member of the S.M.C.

		Munros (I)	Tops (II)	Furth (III)
1.	*Rev. A. E. Robertson	1901	—	—
2.	*Rev. A. R. G. Burn	1923	1923	—
3.	*J. A. Parker	1927	—	1929
4.	*J. R. Corbett	1930	1930	—
5.	*J. Dow	1933	1947	1956
6.	J. Robertson	1938	—	—
7.	*G. G. Elliot	1938	—	—
8.	*A. L. Cram	1939	1939	—
	and	1978	1978	—
9.	J. Hirst	1947	1947	—
10.	Mrs Hirst	1947	1947	—
11.	*E. W. Hodge	1947	—	—
12.	*B. Horsburgh	1947	—	—
13.	*W. M. Docharty	1948	1948	1949
14.	W. D. McKinlay	1948	—	—
15.	J. Campbell	1949	—	—
16.	*C. V. Dodgson	1951	1951	—
17.	H. Hampton	1952	—	—
18.	*G. S. Ritchie	1953	—	—
19.	J. S. Anderson	1953	1953	1958
20.	*G. G. MacPhee	1954	1955	—
21.	*P. J. L. Heron	1954	—	1956
22.	*J. F. Hamilton	1954	—	1956
23.	*M. Hutchinson	1955	1955	—
24.	E. I. Lawson	1955	1955	—
25.	W. T. Allan	1956	—	—
26.	*J. Mallinson	1956	—	—
27.	*J. Ferrier	1956	—	—
28.	*G. Peat	1957	1967	—
29.	*J. A. Watt	1957	1957	1958
30.	E. Maxwell	1957	1957	1958
	and	1966	1966	—
31.	C. G. Macdonald	1958	—	—
32.	*J. Y. Macdonald	1958	—	—
33.	A. G. McKenzie	1958	—	1969
	and	1980	—	—
34.	J. C. Grant	1959	—	1961
35.	T. P. Kemp	1959	—	—
36.	Mrs J. Ferrier	1960	—	—

		Munros (I)	Tops (II)	Furth (III)
37.	Mrs M. J. Linklater-Shirras.........	1960	—	—
38.	Miss A. J. Littlejohn...............	1960	1960	1960
39.	Miss A. D. Miller..................	1960	—	1961
40.	*T. Nicholson	1960	1961	—
41.	Mrs K. M. Watson	1960	—	—
42.	J. R. Watson	1960	—	—
43.	*J. C. Donaldson	1961	—	—
44.	P. A. Larder......................	1961	—	1961
45.	P. N. L. Tranter	1961	—	—
	and	1964	—	—
46.	*J. C. I. Wedderburn	1962	—	—
47.	J. M. Burnett.....................	1962	—	—
48.	A. E. Robinson	1962	—	—
49.	K. D. Shaw.......................	1962	—	—
50.	Miss L. Ticehurst..................	1962	1962	1962
51.	*K. M. Andrew	1962	1969	—
52.	*G. H. Smith	1962	—	—
53.	*G. M. Smith.....................	1963	1966	1968
	and	1969	1969	1971
54.	*W. L. Wood......................	1963	—	—
55.	I. A. Robertson	1963	—	—
56.	J. Cosgrove	1963	—	—
	and	1974	—	—
57.	*J. N. Ledingham	1963	—	1981
58.	A. Farquharson...................	1963	—	—
59.	*A. R. Thrippleton	1964	—	—
60.	J. G. Fleming.....................	1964	—	—
61.	W. D. Fraser	1964	—	—
62.	*H. M. Brown.....................	1965	1965	1967
	and	1969	—	1969
	and	1970	—	1971
	and	1974	—	1978
	and	1975	—	1979
	and	1979	—	—
63.	*W. T. Taylor	1965	1966	1967
64.	R. M. Milne......................	1965	—	—
65.	H. S. K. Stapley..................	1965	—	1965
66.	R. Hutchison	1965	—	—
67.	G. C. Sime	1966	1966	1969
68.	*W. D. Nichol	1966	—	—
69.	*D. C. H. Green	1966	1966	1969
70.	*G. King.........................	1966	—	—
71.	*D. Barclay	1966	—	—
72.	D. Hawksworth...................	1967	—	1969
73.	A. M. Fraser	1967	1979	1977
	and	1980	—	—
74.	A. C. Gardner	1967	—	1970
75.	Miss M. McCallum	1967	1968	—
76.	Matthew J. Moulton...............	1968	—	—
	and	1971	—	—
	and	1978	—	—

		Munros (I)	Tops (II)	Furth (III)
76.	Matthew J. Moulton	1980	—	—
	and	1982	—	—
77.	R. Smith	1968	1968	—
78.	Miss L. W. Urquhart	1968	—	—
79.	Mrs E. MacKay	1968	—	—
80.	A. J. Main	1968	—	—
81.	*R. D. Walton	1968	—	—
82.	W. Shand	1968	1968	1969
83.	G. G. Shand	1968	1968	1971
84.	R. L. Pearce	1968	—	—
85.	Barbara M. Tulloch	1968	—	—
86.	Helen M. Scrimgeour	1968	—	—
87.	*J. Hinde	1968	—	—
88.	R. W. G. Wood	1969	—	—
89.	I. T. Stephen	1969	—	—
90.	R. J. Grant	1969	—	—
91.	*W. T. Tauber	1969	—	—
92.	R. Hainsworth	1969	1969	—
93.	K. R. Cox	1969	1969	1983
94.	R. Armour	1969	—	—
	and	1980	—	—
95.	Mrs E. R. Innes	1969	—	—
96.	W. G. Carter	1969	1970	1971
	and	1980	—	—
97.	B. Finlayson	1970	—	—
98.	*G. Chisholm	1970	—	—
99.	J. W. Brydie	1970	—	—
100.	*M. G. Geddes	1970	1970	—
101.	R. Gilbert	1971	—	—
102.	G. Downs	1971	—	—
103.	P. Edwards	1971	1980	1980
104.	I. Rae	1971	—	—
105.	I. Butterfield	1971	—	—
106.	J. Gillies	1971	—	—
107.	*Andrew Nisbet	1972	—	—
108.	B. K. E. Edridge	1972	—	—
	and	1982	—	—
109.	*G. S. Roger	1972	—	—
110.	Colin Turner	1973	1973	—
111.	R. Cook	1973	1973	1973
112.	P. Roberts	1973	1975	—
113.	W. G. Barbour	1973	—	—
114.	D. Smith	1973	1982	—
115.	K. MacLean	1973	—	—
116.	A. Robertson	1973	—	—
117.	J. Dawson	1973	—	—
118.	Diane Stadring	1973	—	—
119.	Janet Clark	1973	—	—
120.	John Mills	1973	—	—
121.	Don Smithies	1973	—	—
122.	W. C. T. Sarson	1973	1973	—

		Munros (I)	Tops (II)	Furth (III)
123.	A. L. Mackenzie	1973	—	—
124.	Archibald G. H. Grant	1973	—	—
125.	A. R. Dunn	1974	—	—
126.	A. E. Lawson	1974	1974	1976
127.	D. J. Farrant	1974	—	—
128.	R. Hardie	1974	—	—
129.	*J. W. Simpson	1974	—	—
130.	J. Sloane	1974	—	—
131.	L. MacKenzie	1975	—	—
132.	R. Millar	1975	—	—
133.	*F. R. Wylie	1975	—	1981
134.	C. Marsden	1976	—	—
135.	D. Hunter	1976	—	—
136.	R. L. St. C. Murray	1976	1980	1980
137.	I. C. Spence	1976	—	—
138.	R. Payne	1976	—	—
139.	W. Douglas	1976	—	—
140.	M. Keates	1976	—	—
141.	E. Pilling	1976	—	—
142.	R. Morgan	1976	1976	1977
143.	A. E. Law	1976	1983	—
144.	D. Tooke	1976	—	—
145.	R. Graham	1976	—	—
146.	*Campbell R. Steven	1976	—	—
147.	R. Davie	1976	—	—
148.	D. Whalley	1976	—	—
149.	T. MacDonald	1976	—	—
150.	D. Henderson	1976	—	—
151.	Murdo E. Macdonald	1977	—	—
152.	Erland Flett	1977	—	—
153.	A. N. Darbyshire	1977	—	—
154.	Jock Murray	1977	—	—
155.	Edward F. Emley	1977	—	1980
156.	R. D. Leitch	1977	—	—
157.	*W. Myles	1977	—	—
158.	M. H. MacKinnon	1977	—	—
159.	Denise Marsden	1977	1977	—
160.	W. A. Donaldson	1977	—	—
161.	A. F. des Moulins	1977	—	—
	and	1981	—	—
162.	Duncan C. Gray	1978	—	—
163.	Iain G. Gray	1978	—	—
164.	N. Hawkins	1978	—	—
165.	J. L. Morning	1978	—	—
166.	T. Moore	1978	—	—
167.	J. Allan	1978	—	—
168.	S. Robertson	1978	—	—
169.	A. S. Bowie	1978	—	—
170.	J. E. Smith	1978	—	—
171.	F. Wiley	1978	—	—
172.	I. C. Murray	1978	—	—

		Munros (I)	Tops (II)	Furth (III)
173.	I. C. Munro	1978	1978	—
174.	Mrs Pat Bell	1978	1978	—
175.	A. G. MacLean	1978	1979	1978
176.	S. Craven	1978	—	—
177.	A. F. Craven	1978	—	—
178.	D. A. Shanks	1978	—	—
179.	R. C. Munro	1978	1978	—
180.	J. Stewart	1978	—	—
181.	Mrs A. L. Cram	1978	1978	—
182.	W. Steele	1978	—	—
183.	A. Stevens	1978	—	—
184.	S. Beck	1978	—	—
185.	Susan Mackenzie	1978	—	—
186.	C. E. Barton	1979	—	—
187.	Sue Robertson	1979	—	—
188.	D. A. Peet	1979	—	—
189.	David Lane	1979	—	—
190.	A. L. Bartlet	1979	—	1979
191.	P. Cooper	1979	1979	1976
192.	Carole Smithies	1979	—	—
193.	Pamela Brown	1979	—	—
194.	P. D. Brown	1979	—	—
195.	Leonard Jameson	1979	—	—
196.	M. R. Don	1979	—	—
197.	John Rogers	1979	—	—
198.	S. R. Palmer	1979	—	—
199.	Dewi Jones	1979	—	—
200.	F. Telfer	1979	—	—
201.	Mrs M. Tildesley	1979	—	—
202.	H. Thomson	1979	—	—
203.	D. Foster	1979	—	—
204.	Christopher Bond	1980	—	—
205.	Tom Rix	1980	—	1983
206.	I. H. Chuter	1980	—	—
207.	*Ivan Waller	1980	1981	—
208.	Brian D. Batty	1980	—	—
209.	Patricia Batty	1980	—	—

Henceforward late entries are recorded according to date of receipt irrespective of date of "compleation".

		Munros (I)	Tops (II)	Furth (III)
210.	Archie Mitchell	1973	—	—
211.	Fergus McIntosh	1979	1980	1980
212.	W. Ross Napier	1980	—	—
213.	Ronald Leask	1980	1980	—
214.	Sue Jardine	1980	—	—
215.	D. Alistair Baird	1980	—	—
216.	Jeremy Fenton	1980	—	—
217.	J. R. M. Lubbock	1976	—	—
218.	P. D. Binnie	1977	—	—
219.	*R. Hillcoat	1980	—	—

		Munros (I)	Tops (II)	Furth (III)
220.	Peter Edward	1980	—	—
221.	Raymond Hutcheson	1980	—	—
222.	Ronald Crawford	1980	—	—
223.	Carole M. Davie	1980	—	—
224.	Stanley Grant	1980	—	—
225.	Alan L. Brook	1980	1980	1978
226.	M. W. McCue	1980	1980	1980
227.	*Donald Mill	1980	—	—
228.	Alan Gately	1980	—	—
229.	Stan Bradshaw	1980	1980	1980
230.	John Howarth	1980	1980	1980
231.	C. R. Knowles	1980	1980	—
232.	*Trevor Ransley	1980	—	—
233.	Sheila Cormack	1980	—	—
234.	Anne McGeachie	1980	—	—
235.	George McGeachie	1980	—	—
236.	R. W. J. Webster	1981	—	—
237.	*Haswell Oldham	1969	1972	1961
238.	Connie Thompson	1980	—	—
239.	Frank Tildesley	1980	—	—
240.	Mike Lidwell	1980	1980	—
241.	Roger Clarke	1980	—	—
242.	Rona M. Craig	1981	—	—
243.	Fiona M. Wilkie	1981	—	—
244.	*Roger O'Donovan	1981	—	—
245.	David A. Williams	1981	—	—
246.	John M. Dunn	1981	—	—
247.	K. J. Hay	1981	1982	1982
248.	W. L. Wyllie	1981	—	—
249.	Andrew Martin	1981	—	—
250.	Leonard Moss	1981	—	—
251.	Christopher Townsend	1981	—	—
252.	Elizabeth M. Devenay	1981	—	—
253.	William T. Devenay	1981	—	—
254.	*James Renny	1981	—	—
255.	W. D. Duncan	1981	—	—
256.	H. F. Barron	1981	—	—
257.	John Colls	1981	—	—
258.	I. R. W. Park	1981	—	—
259.	D. A. Bearhop	1981	—	—
260.	Geraldine Guestsmith	1981	—	—
261.	Robert I. Scott	1981	—	—
262.	*Roger Robb	1981	—	—
263.	James Boyd	1981	—	—
264.	Donn Vass	1981	—	—
265.	G. H. Maynard	1981	—	—
266.	Norman McDonald	1965	—	1966
267.	Martin Hudson	1981	1981	1982
268.	Patience Barton	1982	—	—
269.	Winnie Reid	1982	—	—
271.	David Reid	1982	—	—

		Munros (I)	Tops (II)	Furth (III)
272.	Robert Durran.....................	1982	—	—
273.	A. M. Snodgrass	1982	—	—
274.	Edward MacGregor	1982	—	—
275.	David Phillips	1982	1982	—
276.	THE UNKNOWN MUNROIST† ...	—	—	—
277.	Gerry Knight	1982	1982	1983
278.	Ewan C. Douglas..................	1982	—	—
279.	Donald Ross......................	1982	—	—
280.	Jim Wyllie	1982	—	—
281.	Chris Andrews.....................	1982	—	—
282.	Christine Dale	1982	—	—
283.	Michael Dale	1983	—	—
284.	Simon Dale.......................	1982	—	—
285.	J. L. Campbell....................	1982	—	—
286.	Donald McCall	1982	—	—
287.	Catherine MacMillan	1982	—	—
288.	Jim Braid	1982	1982	—
289.	D. L. Sands	1982	1982	—
290.	Kenneth J. MacIver................	1982	—	—
291.	Donald MacLeod Duthie	1982	—	—
292.	Kathy Murgatroyd	1982	—	—
293.	W. G. Park.......................	1982	1982	—
294.	D. M. Inglis	1982	1982	—
295.	Wm. A. Mitchell	1982	—	—
296.	John E. Ramsay	1983	—	1982
297.	Duncan MacNiven	1983	—	—
298.	Ian Bryce	1983	—	—
299.	L. J. Skuodas.....................	1983	—	—
300.	*Derek G. Pyper	1983	—	—
301.	R. D. Whittal.....................	1983	—	—
302.	Alan C. Sloan	1983	1983	1983
303.	Neil C. Cromar	1983	—	—
304.	E. Martin	1983	—	—

†*There is an explanation of this entry in the S.M.C. Journal for 1983.*

THE LOST LEADER

(A cautionary tale for Munroists)
with apologies to Browning.

Just for a handful of summits he left us,
Just for a "Dearg" to tick on his list.
Thus Munro's Tables have slowly bereft us,
Changed Ultramontane to Salvationist.
Raeburn was with us, Collie was of us,
Ling, Glover were for us—they watch from belays.
He alone breaks from the van and the freemen,
Climbs up his mountains the easiest ways.

We shall climb prospering—not thro' his presence,
Leads will inspirit us—not on his rope.
Deeds will be done while he boasts his collection,
Ben Vane to Braeriach, Mount Keen to Ben Hope.
Blot out his name then, record one lost soul more,
One more peak-bagger to collar them all.
Pelt him with pitons and crown him with crampons,
Leave him spreadeagled on Rubicon Wall!

D.J.F.

Corbett's Tables

SCOTTISH MOUNTAINS 2500 FEET
AND UNDER 3000 FEET IN HEIGHT
WITH RE-ASCENT OF 500 FEET ON ALL SIDES

by J. ROOKE CORBETT

Edited and revised by J. C. Donaldson and Hamish M. Brown

1984 revision by J. C. Donaldson

FOREWORD

J. ROOKE CORBETT did not publish his List of 2500-feet mountains, all of which he himself had ascended, probably because he felt that before doing so some further checking on the ground would be desirable. After his death it was passed by his sister to the Guide Books General Editor, who decided that it was worthy of record as of interest and assistance to hill walkers generally, and it was printed as he left it subject to some minor amendments.

There was no indication in Corbett's papers as to the criterion he adopted in listing the heights included, but it seems clear that his only test was a re-ascent of 500 feet on all sides to every point admitted, no account being taken of distance or difficulty. A detailed check of the latest maps has been made for this Edition resulting in 17 peaks being added to the List while 11 have been removed from it. The Section numbering has been revised, listing first areas south of the Great Glen, then those to the north followed by the Islands. In each Section the hills are placed in a mainly south to north order. 762m is taken as the equivalent of 2500 feet but, as O.S. figures are to the nearest metre only, a hill given a height of 762m on an O.S. map cannot be accepted as a Corbett without checking that the exact height is not below 762m.

The List remains not strictly comparable with those compiled by either Munro or Donald as it does not profess to include all "summits" and "tops" from 2500 to 2999 feet, which on a Munro or Donald basis would give a much larger total.

Kirriereoch Hill and Cramalt Craig have been deleted, there no longer being a 500 feet re-ascent on all sides according to the latest O.S. map.

Sron a' Choire Chnapanich in Section 4 has been added to the list. It is named in the 1:25,000 map with a height of 837m as compared with only 686c in the 1:50,000.

Beinn Each has been added in Sec. 2. The 1:25,000 map gives a height of 813m. and the contours are different giving a re-ascent of over 500m.

The revisions of 1984 make the changes from the 1974 edition 13 removed and 19 added.

Heights taken from 1:25,000 are marked by a †.

Changes made to the 1974 Edition

Number listed in the 1974 Edition of the Tables   217

Removed from List in this Edition:

Old Section No.	5b	Beinn Chumhain. Does not have a re-ascent of 500 feet on all sides.
	6	Carn Easgann Bana. Does not have a re-ascent of 500 feet on all sides.
		Carn na Laraiche Maoile. Height now exceeded by that of Carn na Saobhaide, formerly of equal status.
	7a	Druim Garbh. Does not have a re-ascent of 500 feet on all sides.
	7b	Druim Fiaclach. Replaced by Sgurr na Ba Glaise.
	7c	Beinn an Tuim. Does not have a re-ascent of 500 feet on all sides.
		Meall Coire nan Saobhaidh. Replaced by Meall na h-Eilde.
	7d	Bhuidhe Bheinn. Replaced by Sgurr a' Bhac Chaolais.
	9	Sgurr nan Ceannaichean. Promoted to Munro status.
	15	Sgor Mor. Does not have a re-ascent of 500 feet on all sides.
		Meall Uaine. Does not have a re-ascent of 500 feet on all sides.
New Section No.	1	Kirriereoch Hill
		Cramalt Craig

Total removed   13

204

Added to List in this Edition:

New Section No.	2	Beinn an Lochain. Reduced from Munro.
		Beinn Each.
	3	Cam Chreag.
	4	Sron a' Choire Chnapanich.
	5	Meall Ligiche.
	6	Sow of Atholl.
		Meall na Meoig of Ben Pharlagain.
	9	Corrieyairack Hill. Equal height with Gairbeinn.
	10	Beinn na Uamha.
		Sgurr na Ba Glaise. In place of Druim Fiaclach.
		Beinn Mhic Cedidh.
	11	Sgurr Cos na Breachd-Laoidh.
		Sgurr a' Bhac Chaolais. In place of Bhuidhe Bheinn.
	12	Meall na h-Eilde. In place of Meall Coire nan Saobhaidh.
	14	Sgurr Gaorsaic.
	15	Beinn Liath Mhor a' Ghiubhais Li.
		Little Wyvis.
	16	Sail Gorm, Quinag.
	18	Beinn Talaidh, Mull.

Total added   19

Total number of Corbetts in this Edition   223

SCOTTISH MOUNTAINS OF 2500 FEET
AND UNDER 3000 FEET IN HEIGHT
WITH RE-ASCENT OF 500 FEET ON ALL SIDES

Name	Height	Map Sht. Nos. O.S.	Map Sht. Nos. Bart.	Map Reference

SECTION 1

South of the Forth-Clyde Canal

	Name	Height	O.S.	Bart.	Map Reference
1.	Shalloch on Minnoch	768	77	37/40	405907
2.	Merrick	843	77	37	428855
3.	Corserine	814	77	37/40	497871
4.	Cairnsmore of Carsphairn	797	77	40	594980
5.	Hart Fell	808	78	40/41	114136
6.	White Coomb	822	79	41	163151
7.	Broad Law	840	72	41	146235

SECTION 2

Loch Fyne to Balquhidder and Loch Earn

	Name	Height	O.S.	Bart.	Map Reference
1.	Beinn Bheula	779	56	44	155983
2.	Ben Donich	847	56	44/48	218043
3.	The Brack	787	56	44/48	246031
4.	Ben Arthur (The Cobbler)	884	56	44/48	259058
5.	Beinn Luibhean	858	56	—	243079
6.	Beinn an Lochain	901	56	48	218079
7.	Binnein an Fhidhleir	817*	56/50	48	230109
8.	Meall an Fhudair	764	56/50	48	271192
9.	Beinn a' Choin	770	56/50	48	354130
10.	Stob a' Choin	865	56	48	416161
11.	Ceann na Baintighearna**	771	57	48	474163
12.	Benvane	821	57	48	535137
13.	Ben Ledi	879	57	48	562098
14.	Beinn Each	813†	57	48	602158
15.	Meall na Fearna	809	57	48	651186

*The highest point is 1500m east of the name on the map.
**Highest point lies 1400m south of name on map.

Name	Height	Map Sht. Nos. O.S.	Bart.	Map Reference

SECTION 3

Loch Etive, Glen Orchy and Auch

	Name	Height	O.S.	Bart.	Map Reference
1.	Beinn a' Bhuiridh	897	50	47	094283
2.	Beinn Chuirn	880	50	48	281292
3.	Beinn Mhic-Mhonaidh	792†	50	48/47	209350
4.	Beinn Udlaidh	840	50	48	280333
5.	Beinn Bhreac-liath	803	50	48	304339
6.	Beinn Odhar	900	50	48	338338
7.	Beinn Chaorach	818	50	48	359328
8.	Cam Chreag	885††	50	48	375346
9.	Beinn a' Chaisteil	885†	50	48	348364
10.	Beinn nam Fuaran	807†	50	48	361382
11.	Creach Bheinn	810	50	47	024422
12.	Beinn Trilleachan	840c†	50	47	086439
13.	Stob Dubh, Beinn Ceitlein	883	50	47/48	166488

††*Height from 1:25,000 O.S. There is, therefore, a re-ascent of 500 feet on all sides.*

SECTION 4

Glen Lyon, Breadalbane and Glenalmond

	Name	Height	O.S.	Bart.	Map Reference
1.	Beinn nan Imirean	844	51	48	419309
2.	Meall an t-Seallaidh	852	51	48	542234
3.	Creag MacRanaich	809	51	48	546256
4.	Creag Uchdag	879	51	48/52	708323
5.	Creagan na Beinne	887	51	48/52	744369
6.	Meall Luaidhe[1]	780	51	48	586436
7.	Beinn nan Oighreag	909	51	48	543414
8.	Meall nan Subh	804	51	48	461397
9.	Sron a' Choire Chnapanich	837†	51	48	456453
10.	Meall Buidhe[2]	907	51	48	426449
11.	Cam Chreag	862	51	48	536491
12.	Beinn Dearg	830	51	48	609497
13.	Auchnafree Hill	789†	52	48	809309
14.	Meall Tairneachan	787	52	48	807544
15.	Farragon Hill	783	52	48	840553

1. Meall nan Maigheach on 1:25,000 779m.

2. 900c. only in 1:25,000.

SECTION 5

Appin and Etive to Glen Spean

	Name	Height	O.S.	Bart.	Map Reference
1.	Fraochaidh	879	41	47	029517
2.	Meall Lighiche	772	41	47	094528
3.	Beinn Maol Chaluim	904	41	47/48	135526

Name	Height	Map Sht. Nos. O.S.	Map Sht. Nos. Bart.	Map Reference

SECTION 5 *(continued)*

	Name	Height	O.S.	Bart.	Map Reference
4.	Beinn Mhic Chasgaig	862	41	47/48	221502
5.	Beinn a' Chrulaiste	857	41	50/48	246567
6.	Garbh Bheinn	867	41	50/51	169601
7.	Mam na Gualainn	796	41	50/47	115625
8.	Glas Bheinn	789	41	50/48	259641
9.	Leum Uilleim.....................	906	41	51/48	331641
10.	Sgurr Innse......................	808	41	50/51	290748
11.	Cruach Innse	857	41	50/51	280763

SECTION 6

Loch Rannoch to Loch Laggan and Badenoch

	Name	Height	O.S.	Bart.	Map Reference
1.	Meall na Meoig of Ben Pharlagain ...	868	42	51/48	448642
2.	Stob an Aonaich Mhoir	855	42	51	537694
3.	Beinn Mholach	841	42	51/48	587655
4.	Beinn a' Chuallaich................	892	42	51/48	684618
5.	Meall na Leitreach................	775	42	51	639703
6.	The Sow of Atholl................	803	42	51	624741
7.	The Fara........................	911	42	51	598844
8.	An Dun..........................	827	42	51	716802
9.	Craig an Loch	876	42	51	735807
10.	Meallach Mhor	769	35	51	777909
11.	Carn Dearg Mor	857	35	51	824912

SECTION 7

Atholl, Glen Feshie, Glen Shee and Deeside

	Name	Height	O.S.	Bart.	Map Reference
1.	Ben Vrackie	841	43	51/48	951632
2.	Ben Vuirich	903	43	51/52	997700
3.	Ben Gulabin.....................	806	43	51/52	101722
4.	Monamenach.....................	807	43	52	176707
5.	Beinn Mheadhonach...............	901	43	—	880758
6.	Beinn Bhreac	912	43	51	868821
7.	Leathad an Taobhain	912	43	51	822858
8.	Sgor Mor (Glen Dee)..............	813	43	51/52	006914
9.	Creag nan Gabhar.................	834	43	51/52	154841
10.	Morrone........................	859	43	51/52	132886
11.	Conachcraig.....................	865	44	52	280865
12.	Ben Tirran	896	44	52	373746
13.	Mount Battock	778	44	52	550844

Name	Height	Map Sht. Nos. O.S.	Map Sht. Nos. Bart.	Map Reference

SECTION 7 *(continued)*

	Name	Height	O.S.	Bart.	Reference
14.	Carn na Drochaide	818	36/43	52/51	127938
15.	Creag an Dail Bheag*	862	36/43	52/51	158981
16.	Culardoch	900	36/43	52	193988
17.	Brown Cow Hill...................	829	36	52	221044
18.	Morven..........................	871	37	52	377040

Carn Liath at MR 165977 is also 862m and is more prominent from Braemar.

SECTION 8

Avon, Don and Rinnes

	Name	Height	O.S.	Bart.	Reference
1.	Creag Mhor	895	36	51/52	057048
2.	Meall a' Bhuachaille	810	36	51/52/55	991115
3.	Geal Charn.......................	821	36	51/52/55	090127
4.	Carn Ealasaid	792	36	52/56	228118
5.	Carn Mor	804	37	52/56	265183
6.	Cook's Cairn	774*	37	56	299275
7.	Corryhabbie Hill	781	37	56	281289
8.	Ben Rinnes†	840	28	56	255355

400m south-east from the point where the name appears on the map.
†*On the map the highest point of Ben Rinnes is named Scurran of Lochterlandoch. This name is also given on Bartholomew's map.*

SECTION 9

Glen Roy, Corrieyairack and the Monadh Liath

	Name	Height	O.S.	Bart.	Reference
1.	Beinn Iaruinn....................	800c	34	50/51	296900
2.	Carn Dearg (south of Glen Roy)	834	34	51/41	345887
3.	Beinn Teallach...................	913	34	51/41	361859
4.	Carn Dearg (north of Glen Roy)	768	34	51	357948
5.	Carn Dearg (Gleann Eachach).......	815	34	51	349967
6.	Gairbeinn.......................	896	34	51	460985
7.	Corrieyairack Hill	896	34	51	429998
8.	Carn a'Chuilinn...................	816	34	51	416034
9.	Meall na h-Aisre	862	35	51	515000
10.	Carn na Saobhaidhe	811	35	51	600145
11.	Carn an Fhreiceadain	878	35	51	726071
12.	Geal-charn Mor..................	824	35	51	837124

SECTION 10

Loch Linnhe to Lochailort and Glenfinnan

	Name	Height	O.S.	Bart.	Reference
1.	Fuar Bheinn.....................	766	49	47	853564
2.	Creach Bheinn...................	853	49	47/50	871577
3.	Garbh Bheinn	885	40	47/50	904622
4.	Beinn Resipol....................	845	40	50	766655

Name	Height	Map Sht. Nos. O.S.	Bart.	Map Reference

SECTION 10 *(Continued)*

	Name	Height	O.S.	Bart.	Map Reference
5.	Beinn na h-Uamha	762†	40	50	918665
6.	Sgurr Dhomhnuill	888	40	50	889679
7.	Carn na Nathrach	786	40	50	887699
8.	Rois-Bheinn	882	40	50	756778
9.	Sgurr na Ba Glaise	874	40	50	770777
10.	An Stac	814	40	50	763793
11.	Beinn Mhic Cedidh	783	40	50	829788
12.	Beinn Odhar Bheag	882	40	50	846778
13.	Druim Tarsuinn	770	40	50	875727
14.	Sgurr Ghiubhsachain	849	40	50	876751
15.	Sgorr Craobh a' Chaorainn	775	40	50	895758
16.	Sgurr an Utha	796	40	50	885839
17.	Streap	909	40	50	946863
18.	Braigh nan Uamhachan	765	40	50	975867
19.	Stob Coire a' Chearcaill	771†	41	—	017727
20.	Meall a' Phubuill	774	41	50	029854

†*Most precise height available from O.S. who state that if it had been plotted originally in imperial units it would have been published as 2500 ft.*

SECTION 11

Loch Morar to Glen Shiel

	Name	Height	O.S.	Bart.	Map Reference
1.	Carn Mor	829	33	50	903910
2.	Sgurr na h-Aide	867†	33	50	889931
3.	Sgurr Cos na Breachd-laoidh*	835	33	50	948947
4.	Fraoch Bheinn	858	33	50	986940
5.	Sgurr Mhurlagain	880†	33	50	012944
6.	Sgurr an Fhuarain	901	33	50	987980
7.	Ben Aden	887	33	50	899986
8.	Beinn Bhuidhe	855	33	50	822967
9.	Sgurr Coire Choinnichean	796	33	50	791011
10.	Beinn na Caillich	785	33	50	796067
11.	Sgurr a' Choire-bheithe	913	33	50	895015
12.	Sgurr nan Eugallt	894	33	50	931045
13.	Sgurr a' Bhac Chaolais	885	33	50/54	958110
14.	Beinn na h-Eaglaise	804	33	50/54	854120
15.	Beinn nan Caorach	773	33	50/54	871122
16.	Sgurr Mhic Bharraich	781†	33	50/54	917174
17.	Am Bathach	798	33	50	073144

Possibly an O.S. misprint for laoigh.

†*Point 867 on the 1:25,000 map is called Bidein a' Chabhair and the western top, 859, is called Sgurr na h-Aide.*

Name	Height	Map Sht. Nos. O.S.	Bart.	Map Reference

SECTION 12

Loch Lochy, Loch Cluanie and Gleann Fhada

	Name	Height	O.S.	Bart.	Map Reference
1.	Beinn Bhan......................	796	34/41	50	141857
2.	Geal Charn......................	804	34	50	156943
3.	Meall na h-Eilde	838	34	50	185946
4.	Ben Tee.........................	901	34	50	241972
5.	Meall Dubh	788	34	50	245078
6.	Druim nan Cnamh	790†	34	50	131077
7.	Carn a' Choire Ghairbh	863	34	50/55	137189
8.	Aonach Shasuinn	889	34	50/55	173180

SECTION 13

Applecross and Torridon

	Name	Height	O.S.	Bart.	Map Reference
1.	Sgurr a' Chaorachain†............	792	24	54	797417
2.	Beinn Bhan......................	896	24	54	804450
3.	Beinn Damh.....................	902	24	54	893502
4.	Beinn Dearg	914*	24	54	895608

*Exact height is 2998 ft.
†Spelt Ghaorachain in 1:50,000 map.

SECTION 14

Loch Duich, Strathcarron and Glen Strathfarrar

	Name	Height	O.S.	Bart.	Map Reference
1.	Sgurr Gaorsaic..................	838c†	25/33	54	036219
2.	Sgurr an Airgid	841	25/33	54	940227
3.	Sguman Coinntich................	879	25	54	977304
4.	Faochaig........................	868	25	54	022317
5.	Aonach Buidhe	899	25	54	058324
6.	Sgorr na Diollaid.................	818	25	55	282362
7.	Beinn Dronaig	797	25	54	037382
8.	Beinn Tharsuinn	863	25	54	055433
9.	Sgurr na Feartaig.................	862	25	54	055454
10.	An Ruadh-stac...................	892	25	54	922481
11.	Fuar Tholl	907	25	54	975489
12.	Sgorr nan Lochan Uaine...........	873	25	54	969531
13.	Sgurr Dubh	782	25	54	979558
14.	An Sidhean......................	814	25	55	171454
15.	Bac an Eich	849	25	55	222489
16.	Meallan nan Uan.................	840	25	—	264545
17.	Sgurr a' Mhuilinn	879	25	55	265558

Name	Height	Map Sht. Nos. O.S.	Bart.	Map Reference

SECTION 14 *(continued)*

Name	Height	O.S.	Bart.	Map Reference
18. Beinn a' Bha'ach Ard	862	26	55	361435

SECTION 15

Loch Maree, Braemore, Freevater and Diebidale to Wyvis

Name	Height	O.S.	Bart.	Map Reference
1. Baosbheinn	875	19/24	54	871654
2. Beinn an Eoin	855	19	54	905646
3. Ruadh-stac Beag	896	19	54	973614
4. Meall a' Ghiubhais	880c	19	54	976634
5. Beinn Airigh Charr	791	19	58	930762
6. Beinn Lair	860	19	54/58	982732
7. Creag Rainich	807	19	58	097751
8. Beinn a' Chaisgein Mor	857	19	58	983785
9. Beinn Dearg Mor.................	908	19	58	032799
10. Beinn Dearg Bheag	818	19	58	020811
11. Sail Mhor......................	767	19	58	033887
12. Beinn Liath Mhor a' Ghiubhais Li ...	766	20	55/59	281713
13. Beinn Enaiglair	889	20	58/59	225805
14. Beinn a' Chaisteil	787	20	59	370801
15. Carn Ban	845	20	58/59	339876
16. Carn Chuinneag	838	20	59	484833
17. Little Wyvis	764	20	55	430645

SECTION 16

Coigach, Assynt and Loch Merkland

Name	Height	O.S.	Bart.	Map Reference
1. Cul Beag.......................	769	15	58	140088
2. Cul Mor	849	15	58	162119
3. Canisp.........................	846	15	58/59	203187
4. Creag Liath	814	15	58/59	287158
5. Glas Bheinn	776	15	58/59	255265
6. Spidean Coinich, Quinag	764	15	58/59	205278
7. Sail Gharbh, Quinag..............	808	15	58/59	209292
8. Sail Gorm, Quinag	776	15	58/59	198304
9. Beinn Leoid	792	15	58/59	320295
10. Meallan Liath Coire Mhic Dhughaill .	801	15	58	357392
11. Ben Hee	873	16	60	426339

Name	Height	Map Sht. Nos.		Map Reference
		O.S.	*Bart.*	

SECTION 17

The Far North

	Name	Height	O.S.	Bart.	Map Reference
1.	Arkle........................	787	9	58	303462
2.	Meall Horn.....................	777	9	58	353449
3.	Ganu Mor, Foinaven	908	9	58	317507
4.	Cranstackie	800	9	58	351556
5.	Beinn Spionnaidh	772	9	58	362573
6.	Ben Loyal.....................	764	10	60	578489

SECTION 18

The Islands

	Name	Height	O.S.	Bart.	Map Reference
	HARRIS				
1.	Clisham	799	13/14	57	155073
	SKYE				
2.	Glamaig	775	32	54	514300
3.	Garbh-bheinn	806	32	54	531232
	RHUM				
4.	Askival......................	812	39	50	393952
5.	Ainshval.....................	781	39	50	379944
	MULL				
6.	Beinn Talaidh	762†	49	47	625347
7.	Dun da Ghaoithe..............	766	49	47	672362
	JURA				
	Paps of Jura—................				
8.	Beinn an Oir.................	784	61	43	498749
	ARRAN				
9.	Goat Fell....................	874	69	44	991415
10.	Beinn Tarsuinn	825	69	44	959412
11.	Cir Mhor	798	69	44	973432
12.	Caisteal Abhail	859	69	44	969444

†*Beinn Talaidh. Highest point lies 25m south west of the pillar and is 2502 ft.*

Donald's Tables

ALL HILLS IN THE SCOTTISH LOWLANDS 2000 FEET IN HEIGHT AND ABOVE

by PERCY DONALD, B.Sc.

Revised by J. C. Donaldson and Hamish M. Brown

1984 revision by J. C. Donaldson

INTRODUCTION

Mr Percy Donald visited every elevation of 2000 feet and over at least once before issuing his Tables and he discarded many of the points examined as unworthy of inclusion as "Tops". His method of determining "Hills" and "Tops" is described in the Explanation of Tables.

The editors' revision is based on the latest O.S. 1:50,000 maps available but where they do not provide essential information reference has been made to larger scale maps. A further review was made in 1983 with changes as noted below. There are now 28 points in the appendix.

The total number of "Hills" is 87 and of "Tops" 138. The most northerly hill is Innerdownie in the Ochils, the most easterly† Cairn Hill (not named on any map) on The Cheviot, if tops are considered, otherwise Windy Gyle in the Cheviots. The most southerly is Cairnsmore of Fleet, and the most westerly Shalloch on Minnoch, both in Galloway (extreme points in the last two cases are actually tops, Knee of Cairnsmore and Shalloch on Minnoch, North Top).

Carlin's Cairn, Sec. 10., has been promoted to separate "Hill".

Three points in the appendix have been made "Tops"—
Sec. 2. Windlestraw Law, South-west Top.
    5. Conscleuch Head.
    9. Keoch Rig.

In Sec. 5 Black Law North-east Top becomes the main peak, the former "Hill" becoming the South-west Top.

Shiel Dod, Jedburgh Knees and Moorbrock Hill have been added to the appendix.

†*Cauldcleuch Head in Roxburgh is the most easterly hill wholly in Scotland.*

EXPLANATION OF TABLES

Table 1

In this Table the following grouping has been adopted:—

Section	Area	Hills	Tops
1	Ochil Hills	5	9
2	Moorfoot Hills	5	6
3	Tinto..	1	1
4	Enclosed by the Biggar-Broughton-Moffat roads	5	8
5	Enclosed by the Broughton-Innerleithen-St Mary's Loch-Tweedsmuir roads..............................	13	22
6	Enclosed by the Tweedsmuir-St Mary's Loch-Moffat roads	10	21
7	Enclosed by the Moffat-St Mary's Loch-Tushielaw-Eskdalemuir roads	9	15
8	Between the Abington-Moffat and New Cumnock-Thornhill roads...................................	12	15
9	Between the New Cumnock-Thornhill and Dalmellington-New Galloway roads..............................	6	11
10	Between the Dalmellington-New Galloway Station and Girvan-Creetown roads	19	26
11	Cauldcleuch Head.................................	1	1
12	Cheviot Hills (on Union Boundary)	1	3
		87	138

Section 12 includes also six hills wholly in England.

An Appendix gives particulars of 28 additional elevations not meriting inclusion as tops, but all enclosed by an isolated 610m (2000-feet) contour. These have been included in order that the Table may be a complete record of every separate area of ground reaching 610m (2000-feet) in accordance with Mr Donald's policy.

Column 1. Name. The Ordnance Survey spelling is always followed, an * implying that the name appears only on the 1:10,000 or 6-inch maps. Where no name appears on any map the top has been given the name of its hill with North, South, etc., Top added. The number in this column is merely for convenience of reference from Tables II and III.

Column 2. Height. Heights are the latest available from the Ordnance Survey, those marked † being taken from large scale metric maps, while ‡ indicates that they are converted imperial heights from Pathfinder maps which are based on modern surveys. 610m have been taken as the equivalent of 2000 feet.

Columns 3 and 4. Hill and top numbers. These give the number in order of altitude of such tops as may be considered separate hills and their subsidiary tops respectively.

"Tops" and "Hills" were determined by Mr Donald in accordance with the following rules:—

"Tops". All elevations with a drop of 100 feet (30.48m) on all sides and elevations of sufficient topographical merit with a drop of between 100 feet and 50 feet (15.24m) on all sides.

"Hills". Grouping of "tops" into "hills", except where inapplicable on topographical grounds, is on the basis that "tops" are not more than 17 units from the main top of the "hill" to which they belong, where a unit is either $\frac{1}{12}$ mile measured along the connecting ridge or one 50-feet contour between the lower "top" and its connecting col.

While the rules as they stand rather lack mathematical precision, the actual result of their application is that, with but few exceptions, an 80-feet (24.38m) drop determines a "top" and the 17-unit rule a "hill".

Columns 5 and 6. Maps. Sheet numbers have been given for the O.S. 1:50,000 and Bartholomew's 1:100,000 maps. It should be borne in mind that there are variations in spellings between the two publications and that heights do not always agree while a number of names are omitted from the latter map.

Column 7. Six figure map references have been used the use of which is explained on all 1:50,000 maps.

The columns giving summit and fences details have been omitted as a great deal of the information is out of date.

Table II

This Table gives the Scottish "hills" and "tops" only (including the three on the Union Boundary), arranged in order of height.

Columns 1 and 2 give the hill and top numbers, as given in columns 3 and 4 of Table I.

Column 3 gives the height. c denotes a contour.

Column 4 gives the name, as given in column 1 of Table I.

Column 5 gives a reference to the Section number and the number of the top in that section so as to enable it to be readily found in Table I.

Table III

This is an alphabetical index to Table I and contains the name of every "hill", "top", and other elevation listed therein.

TABLE I

Name	Height	Hill No.	Top No.	Map Sht. No. O.S.	Map Sht. No. Bart.	Map Reference
SECTION 1—OCHIL HILLS						
1. Blairdenon Hill	631	73	110	58	45/49	866018
2. Ben Ever......................	622	—	122	58	45/49	893001
3. Ben Cleuch....................	721	25	36	58	45/49	903006
4. The Law	638	—	104	58	45/49	910996
5. Andrew Gannel Hill*	670	—	73	58	45/49	919006
6. King's Seat Hill	643	67	94	58	45/49	936998
7. Tarmangie Hill	645	65	92	58	45/49	942014
8. Whitewisp Hill................	643	—	99	58	45/49	955014
9. Innerdownie..................	611	84	132	58	45/49	966031
SECTION 2—MOORFOOT HILLS						
1. Windlestraw Law	659	59	82	73	41	372431
2. Windlestraw Law—S.W. Top	656	—	86	73	41	363421
3. Whitehope Law................	620‡	80	123	73	41	330446
4. Bowbeat Hill	626‡	76	117	73	41	292469
5. Blackhope Scar	651	63	90	73	41	315483
6. Jeffries Corse or Dundreich......	622	79	121	73	41	275491
SECTION 3—TINTO HILLS						
Tinto........................	707	29	44	72	40	953344
SECTION 4—CULTER HILLS						
1. Coomb Dod	635	—	108	72	40	046238
2. Hillshaw Head.................	653	62	89	72	40	048246
3. Gathersnow Hill†	689‡	42	58	72	40	059257
4. Coomb Hill	639	—	102	72	40	069264
5. Hudderstone**	626‡	75	116	72	40	022272
6. Culter Fell	748	14	19	72	40	053291
7. Chapelgill Hill	696	34	52	72	40	068304
8. Cardon Hill	676	—	68	72	40	065315

†*Also named as Glenwhappen Rig on many maps.*
**Formerly named Heatherstone Law.*

Name	Height	Hill No.	Top No.	Map Sht. No. O.S.	Map Sht. No. Bart.	Map Reference
SECTION 5—MANOR HILLS						
1. Talla Cleuch Head* (Muckle Side)	690	41	57	72	41	134218
2. Clockmore	640	—	101	72	41	183229
3. Broad Law	840	2	2	72	41	146235
4. Cramalt Craig	830	3	3	72	41	169248
5. Greenside Law.................	643	68	95	72	41	198256
6. Hunt Law.....................	639	—	103	72	41	150265
7. Fifescar Knowe	809‡	—	7	72	41	176269
8. Dollar Law...................	817	5	5	72	41	178278

Name	Height	Hill No.	Top No.	Map Sht. No. O.S.	Map Sht. No. Bart.	Map Reference
SECTION 5 *(Continued)*						
9. Taberon Law	637	—	105	72	41	146289
10. Middle HIll	715‡	27	41	72	41	159294
11. Drumelzier Law................	668	52	74	72	41	149313
12. Pykestone Hill.................	737	19	24	72	41	173313
13. The Scrape	716	—	40	72	41	176324
14. Deer Law	629	—	112	73	41	223256
15. Conscleuch Head...............	623‡	—	120	73	41	221263
16. Black Law—South-west Top	696	—	51	73	41	218275
17. Black Law†	697‡	35	50	73	41	224280
18. Blackhouse Heights (Black Cleuch Hill)	674‡	—	71	73	41	222290
19. Dun Rig	742‡	17	22	73	41	253316
20. Glenrath Heights (Middle Hill) ...	730‡	22	30	73	41	241323
21. Stob Law	676	48	67	73	41	230333
22. Birkscairn Hill.................	662‡	57	80	73	41	275332

†*Southern end of Blackhouse Heights on 6" map but not named.*

SECTION 6—MOFFAT HILLS

Name	Height	Hill No.	Top No.	Map Sht. No. O.S.	Map Sht. No. Bart.	Map Reference
1. Nether Coomb Craig (Top above).	725‡	—	33	78	—	129110
2. Swatte Fell	730‡	21	29	78	41	118114
3. Falcon Craig* (Top above).......	723	—	34	78	—	123127
4. Saddle Yoke...................	731‡	—	28	78	41	144124
5. Under Saddle Yoke*...........	745	16	21	78	—	143126
6. Hart Fell......................	808	7	8	78	41	114136
7. Whitehope Heights*............	636‡	71	106	78	—	095139
8. Cape Law.......................	721	24	35	78	41	131151
9. Din Law	666‡	—	77	78	41	124157
10. Great Hill	775‡	—	16	78	—	145165
11. Garelet Dod	698‡	31	46	78	41	125173
12. Erie Hill	688‡	43	59	78	41	124188
13. Carlavin Hill	735‡	—	26	78	41	140190
14. Laird's Cleuch Rig* (Top above)..	682	—	62	72	—	125197
15. Carrifran Gans	752‡	—	18	79	41	158137
16. White Coomb	821‡	4	4	79	41	163151
17. Firthhope Rig..................	799‡	—	11	79	41	153154
18. Lochcraig Head................	800	9	10	79	41	167176
19. Molls Cleuch Dod	784‡	12	14	79	41	152180
20. Nickies Knowe.................	761‡	—	17	79	—	164192
21. Garelet Hill	680	—	64	72	—	124201

SECTION 7—ETTRICK HILLS

Name	Height	Hill No.	Top No.	Map Sht. No. O.S.	Map Sht. No. Bart.	Map Reference
1. Loch Fell	688	44	60	79	41	170047
2. West Knowe*..................	655c	—	88	79	—	164053
3. Wind Fell	664	55	78	79	41	179062
4. Hopetoun Craig................	632	—	109	79	—	188068
5. Ettrick Pen....................	692	38	54	79	41	199077
6. Croft Head....................	636	72	107	79	41	153057

Name	Height	Hill No.	Top No.	Map Sht. No. O.S.	Map Sht. No. Bart.	Map Reference
SECTION 7 *(Continued)*						
7. Capel Fell	678	46	65	79	41	164069
8. Smidhope Hill*	643	—	98	79	—	168077
9. White Shank	620	—	125	79	41	169082
10. Bodesbeck Law	664‡	56	79	79	41	169103
11. Mid Rig	615†	—	128	79	41	180123
12. Bell Craig	623‡	77	118	79	41	187129
13. Andrewhinney Hill	678‡	47	66	79	41	198139
14. Trowgrain Middle	627	—	115	79	41	208149
15. Herman Law	614	83	129	79	41	214157
SECTION 8—LOWTHER HILLS						
1. Queensberry	697	33	48	78	40	989998
2. Earncraig Hill	610	87	137	78	40	973013
3. Gana Hill	668	53	75	78	40	954011
4. Wedder Law	666	54	76	78	40	938025
5. Glenleith Fell	611	—	133	78	40	922023
6. Scaw'd Law	661	58	81	78	40	922034
7. Ballencleuch Law	691	40	56	78	40	935049
8. Rodger Law	688	—	61	71/78	40	945058
9. Comb Law	643	69	96	71/78	40	944075
10. Cold Moss	628	—	114	71/78	40	898094
11. East Mount Lowther	631	74	111	71/78	40	877100
12. Lowther Hill	725	23	32	71/78	40	890107
13. Green Lowther	732	20	27	71/78	40	901120
14. Dun Law	675	49	69	71/78	40	917136
15. Lousie Wood Law	618	82	127	71/78	40	932152
SECTION 9—CARSPHAIRN HILLS						
1. Beninner	710	—	43	77	40	606972
2. Cairnsmore of Carsphairn	797	10	12	77	40	595980
3. Moorbrock Hill	651	64	91	77	40	621984
4. Dugland	608†	—	138	77	40	602009
5. Windy Standard	698	32	47	77	40	620015
6. Keoch Rig*	610c	—	136	77	40	618000
7. Alhang	642†	70	100	77	40	643011
8. Alwhat	628†	—	113	77	40	647021
9. Meikledodd Hill	643†	—	97	77	—	661028
10. Blacklorg Hill	681†	45	63	77	40	654043
11. Blackcraig Hill	700	30	45	77	40	648065
SECTION 10—GALLOWAY HILLS						
1. Larg Hill	675	50	70	77	37	425757
2. Lamachan Hill	716	26	38	77	37	435770
3. Curleywee	674	51	72	77	37	454769
4. Millfore	656	61	85	77	37	478755

	Name	Height	Hill No.	Top No.	Map Sht. No. O.S.	Map Sht. No. Bart.	Map Reference
	SECTION 10 *(Continued)*						
5.	Benyellary	719	—	37	77	37	414838
6.	Merrick.......................	843	1	1	77	37	428855
7.	Kirriereoch Hill	786†	11	13	77	37/40	420871
8.	Tarfessock—South Top	620	—	124	77	——	413886
9.	Tarfessock	697	34	49	77	37/40	409892
10.	Shalloch on Minnoch	775†	13	15	77	37/40	407907
11.	Shalloch on Minnoch—North Top	659	—	84	77	—	400920
12.	Craignaw	645	66	93	77	37	459833
13.	Dungeon Hill	610c	86	135	77	37/40	461851
14.	Mullwharchar	692	39	55	77	37/40	454867
15.	Meikle Millyea.................	746	15	20	77	37	518829
16.	Milldown	738	18	23	77	37	510839
17.	Millfire.......................	716	—	39	77	37	508848
18.	Corserine	814	6	6	77	37/40	498871
19.	Carlin's Cairn	807	8	9	77	37/40	497884
20.	Meaul	695	37	53	77	37/40	501910
21.	Cairnsgarroch	659	60	83	77	37/40	515914
22.	Bow..........................	613	—	130	77	37/40	508928
23.	Coran of Portmark	623	78	119	77	37/40	509937
24.	Knee of Cairnsmore	656	—	87	77	37	509654
25.	Cairnsmore of Fleet	711	28	42	77	37	502671
26.	Meikle Mulltaggart	612c	—	131	77	37	512678

SECTION 11—ROXBURGH HILLS

	Name	Height	Hill No.	Top No.	O.S.	Bart.	Map Reference
	Cauldcleuch Head..............	610c	85	134	79	41	458008

SECTION 12—CHEVIOT HILLS
SCOTLAND AND ENGLAND

	Name	Height	Hill No.	Top No.	O.S.	Bart.	Map Reference
1.	Windy Gyle	619	81	126	80	41	855152
2.	Auchope Cairn	726	—	31	80	41	891198
3.	Cairn Hill—West Top...........	737*	—	25	80	41	896193

ENGLAND

	Name	Height	Hill No.	Top No.	O.S.	Bart.	Map Reference
4.	Cairn Hill.....................	776	—	—	80	41	903196
5.	The Cheviot	815	—	—	74	41	909205
6.	Hedgehope Hill	714	—	—	80	41	944197
7.	Comb Fell.....................	650	—	—	80	41	919187
8.	Bloodybush Edge	610	—	—	80	41	902144
9.	Cushat Law	616†	—	—	80	41	928137

The highest point on the Union Boundary. Not named on either O.S. or Bartholomew maps.

SECTION 13—APPENDIX

The following points are not "tops", but each is enclosed by an isolated 610m (2000-ft.) contour. Donald listed 15 of these points. The list now numbers 28 but not all appear on the O.S. 1:50,000 map. Bartholomew map sheet numbers have not been given for this section as few of the points are shown on these maps.

	Name	*Height*	*O.S. Sht. No.*	*Map Reference*
1.	Greenforet Hill*	616	58	862019
2.	White Cleuch Hill	610c‡	73	229298
3.	Birks Hill	624‡	73	282337
4.	Jeffries Corse—North Top	611	73	281495
5.	Shielhope Head or Water Head	612‡	72	191253
6.	Greenside Law—South Top	610c‡	72	197252
7.	Whitehope Knowe*	611‡	78	098144
8.	Ellers Cleuch Rig	610c‡	78	127167
9.	Comb Head	610c	71	902092
10.	Millfore—South-west Top	620	77	472751
11.	Bow—South-west Top	612	77	505925
12.	Bow—Middle Top	610c	77	507927
13.	Shiel Dod	655†	78	947033
14.	Trostan Hill	617†	77	611017
15.	Stake Law	682‡	73	263321
16.	Hundleshope Heights	686c‡	73	250339
17.	Mathieside Cairn	669‡	72	130222
18.	Lamb Knowe	661	72	167225
19.	Tods Knowe	692‡	72	163232
20.	Great Knock	693‡	72	139256
21.	Brown Knowe*	709c‡	72	142249
22.	Notman Law	731‡	72	185260
23.	Long Grain Knowe	703	72	167295
24.	Peden Head	686c	71	906124
25.	Dungrain Law	667	71	911130
26.	Firthybrig Head	764‡	79	158172
27.	Jedburgh Knees	621	77	614027
28.	Moorbrock Hill, North Top	640c	77	615988

TABLE II

THE 2000-FEET TOPS ARRANGED IN ORDER OF ALTITUDE

Hill No.	Top No.	Height	Name	Ref. to Table 1
1	1	843	Merrick...............................	10-6
2	2	840	Broad Law	5-3
3	3	830	Cramalt Craig	5-4
4	4	821‡	White Coomb	6-16
5	5	817	Dollar Law...........................	5-8
6	6	814	Corserine	10-18
—	7	809‡	Fifescar Knowe	5-7
7	8	808	Hart Fell.............................	6-6
8	9	807	Carlin's Cairn	10-19
9	10	800	Lochcraig Head........................	6-18
—	11	799‡	Firthhope Rig.........................	6-17
10	12	797	Cairnsmore of Carsphairn	9-2
11	13	786†	Kirriereoch Hill	10-7
12	14	785‡	Molls Cleuch Dod	6-19
13	15	775	Shalloch on Minnoch	10-10
—	16	775‡	Great Hill............................	6-10
—	17	761‡	Nickies Knowe.........................	6-20
—	18	752‡	Carrifran Gans	6-15
14	19	748	Culter Fell	4-6
15	20	746	Meikle Millyea........................	10-15
16	21	745	Under Saddle Yoke.....................	6-5
17	22	742‡	Dun Rig	5-19
18	23	738	Milldown	10-16
19	24	737	Pykestone Hill.........................	5-12
—	25	737	Cairn Hill (West Top)...................	12-3
—	26	735‡	Carlavin Hill	6-13
20	27	732	Green Lowther.........................	8-13
—	28	731‡	Saddle Yoke...........................	6-4
21	29	730‡	Swatte Fell	6-2
22	30	730‡	Glenrath Heights or Middle Hill	5-20
—	31	726	Auchope Cairn	12-2
23	32	725	Lowther Hill	8-12
—	33	725‡	Nether Coomb Craig (Top above)..........	6-1
—	34	723	Falcon Craig (Top above).................	6-3
24	35	721	Cape Law.............................	6-8
25	36	721	Ben Cleuch...........................	1-3
—	37	719	Benyellary	10-5
26	38	716	Lamachan Hill.........................	10-2
—	39	716	Millfire..............................	10-17
—	40	716	The Scrape	5-13
27	41	715‡	Middle Hill...........................	5-10
28	42	711	Cairnsmore of Fleet	10-25
—	43	710	Beninner.............................	9-1
29	44	707	Tinto................................	3——
30	45	700	Blackcraig Hill........................	9-10

Hill No.	Top No.	Height	Name	Ref. to Table 1
31	46	698‡	Garelet Dod	6-11
32	47	698	Windy Standard	9-5
33	48	697	Queensberry..........................	8-1
34	49	697	Tarfessock	10-9
35	50	697‡	Black Law	5-16
—	51	696	Black Law—South-west Top	5-15
36	52	696	Chapelgill Hill	4-7
37	53	695	Meaul	10-20
38	54	692	Ettrick Pen...........................	7-5
39	55	692	Mullwharchar	10-14
40	56	691	Ballencleuch Law	8-7
41	57	690	Talla Cleuch Head.....................	5-1
42	58	689‡	Gathersnow Hill	4-3
43	59	688‡	Erie Hill	6-12
44	60	688	Loch Fell	7-1
—	61	688	Rodger Law	8-8
—	62	682	Laird's Cleuch Rig* (Top above)..........	6-14
45	63	681†	Blacklorg Hill	9-—
—	64	680	Garelet Hill	6-21
46	65	678	Capel Fell............................	7-7
47	66	678‡	Andrewhinney Hill	7-13
48	67	676	Stob Law	5-2
—	68	676	Cardon Hill	4-8
49	69	675	Dun Law..............................	8-14
50	70	675	Larg Hill.............................	10-1
—	71	674‡	Blackhouse Heights.....................	5-18
51	72	674	Curleywee............................	10-3
—	73	670	Andrew Gannel Hill*	1-5
52	74	668	Drumelzier Law.......................	5-11
53	75	668	Gana Hill	8-3
54	76	666	Wedder Law..........................	8-4
—	77	666‡	Din Law	6-9
55	78	664	Wind Fell	7-3
56	79	664‡	Bodesbeck Law	7-10
57	80	662‡	Birkscairn Hill	5-22
58	81	661	Scaw'd Law	8-6
59	82	659	Windlestraw Law	2-1
60	83	659	Cairnsgarroch	10-21
—	84	659	Shalloch on Minnoch (North Top)	10-11
61	85	656	Millfore	10-4
—	86	656	Windlestraw Law—South-west Top	2-2
—	87	656	Knee of Cairnsmore	10-24
—	88	655c	West Knowe*.........................	7-2
62	89	653	Hillshaw Head.........................	4-2
63	90	651	Blackhope Scar	2-5
64	91	651	Moorbrock Hill........................	9-3
65	92	645	Tarmangie Hill	1-7
66	93	645	Craignaw	10-12
67	94	643	King's Seat Hill	1-6
68	95	643	Greenside Law........................	5-5
69	96	643	Comb Law	8-9

Hill No.	Top No.	Height	Name	Ref. to Table 1
—	97	643†	Meikledodd Hill	9-9
—	98	643	Smidhope Hill*	7-8
—	99	643	Whitewisp Hill.........................	1-8
70	100	642	Alhang	9-7
—	101	640	Clockmore	5-2
—	102	639	Coomb Hill	4-4
—	103	639	Hunt Law.............................	5-6
—	104	638	The Law	1-4
—	105	637	Taberon Law	5-9
71	106	636‡	Whitehope Heights*	6-7
72	107	636	Croft Head............................	7-6
—	108	635	Coomb Dod	4-1
—	109	632	Hopetoun Craig........................	7-4
73	110	631	Blairdenon Hill	1-1
74	111	631	East Mount Lowther....................	8-11
—	112	629	Deer Law	5-14
—	113	628	Alwhat	9-8
—	114	628	Cold Moss	8-10
—	115	627	Trowgrain Middle......................	7-14
75	116	626‡	Hudderstone	4-5
76	117	626‡	Bowbeat Hill	2-4
77	118	623‡	Bell Craig	7-12
78	119	623	Coran of Portmark.....................	10-23
—	120	623‡	Conscleuch Head.......................	5-15
79	121	622	Jeffries Corse.........................	2-6
—	122	622	Ben Ever..............................	1-2
80	123	620‡	Whitehope Law........................	2-3
—	124	620	Tarfessock (South Top)	10-8
—	125	620	White Shank	7-9
81	126	619	Windy Gyle	12-1
82	127	618	Lousie Wood Law......................	8-15
—	128	615	Mid Rig..............................	7-11
83	129	614	Herman Law	7-15
—	130	613	Bow..................................	10-22
—	131	612c	Meikle Mulltaggart	10-26
84	132	611	Innerdownie...........................	1-9
—	133	611	Glenleith Fell	8-5
85	134	610c	Cauldcleuch Head......................	11-—
86	135	610c	Dungeon Hill..........................	10-13
—	136	610c	Keoch Rig* (Windy Standard)............	9-6
87	137	610	Earncraig Hill	8-2
—	138	608†	Dugland	9-4

TABLE III

ALPHABETICAL INDEX TO TABLE I

DISTRICT GUIDE BOOKS TO SCOTLAND

Since the new series S.M.C. district guide books commenced publication in 1968 many requests have been received for an outline of the divisions in Scotland covered by the main series of eight volumes. *Munro's Tables* and the *Mountains of Scotland* are additional volumes in the series covering the whole of Scotland in their respective subjects. The map reproduced on the opposite page shows the eight divisions represented by the main series.

The Scottish Mountaineering Club Journal, published annually in July, is a useful source of additional information about mountaineering in the areas covered by these Tables. Every year it describes new routes and first ascents and reports significant changes in mountain shelters, bridges, paths and general access, as well as alterations to designated mountain heights and the status of Munros and Tops. Additions to the record of Munroists which appears on pages 74 to 79 are published in the S.M.C. Journal.

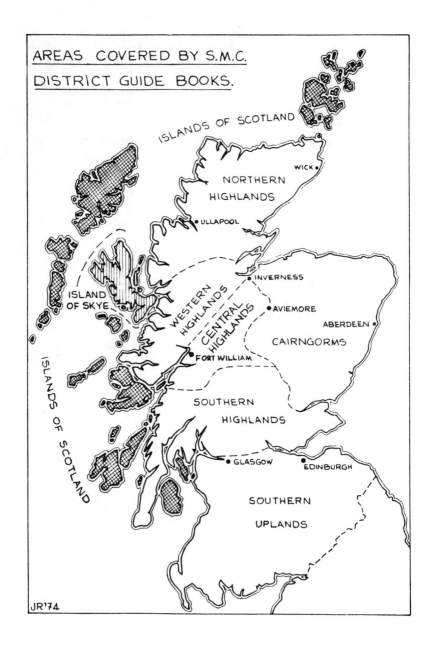

AREAS COVERED BY S.M.C.
DISTRICT GUIDE BOOKS.

ISLANDS OF SCOTLAND

WICK

NORTHERN
HIGHLANDS

ULLAPOOL

INVERNESS

ISLAND
OF SKYE

WESTERN
HIGHLANDS

CENTRAL
HIGHLANDS

AVIEMORE

ABERDEEN

CAIRNGORMS

FORT WILLIAM

ISLANDS OF SCOTLAND

SOUTHERN
HIGHLANDS

GLASGOW

EDINBURGH

SOUTHERN
UPLANDS

JR'74

A Gaelic Guide

TRANSLATIONS AND PRONUNCIATIONS
FOR MUNROS AND TOPS

by Iseabail C. MacLeod and Iain A. MacLeod

Introduction

The vast majority of Scottish mountain names are Gaelic or at least based on Gaelic. In the list (p. 122) we attempt to give those with no knowledge of the language some idea of the meaning and pronunciation of the names of Munros and Tops. Certainty is not always possible: some words have several different meanings and some also vary in meaning from district to district. Others are so old and their forms have changed so much over the centuries that one can only put forward a theory as to their meaning. Where appropriate we have given the source of the speculation, many of them being from the standard work on Gaelic place-names, W. J. Watson's *The History of the Celtic Place-Names of Scotland* (see list of sources, p. 120).

Many of the translations may sound rather strange. This is sometimes because the Gaelic has a connotation which cannot be conveyed in English. For example 'big-hill' for Beinn Mhor (Ben More) does not give the idea of the hill being the most prominent of the local hills. We would be grateful for any suggestions for improvements in the translations.

A simplified pronunciation scheme is included (see p. 119) but it is not intended to be definitive. For example the pronunciation of *beinn* (a hill) is given as [bYn] although you will also hear [bayn] used by Gaelic speakers and [ben] is the commonest pronunciation by non-Gaelic speakers.

We would like to thank many friends and colleagues whose help and advice has been invaluable. We are especially grateful to:

Iain A. Fraser, of the Place-Name Survey, School of Scottish Studies, University of Edinburgh;

Donald Meek, of the Department of Celtic, University of Edinburgh;

Adam Watson, whose forthcoming book, *The Place-Names of Upper Deeside* (to be published by Aberdeen University Press) will give readers more detail information on that area.

For information on particular areas we would like to thank:

Mervyn Browne of Ardtalnaig, Loch Tay; Jean Lindsay of Dundonell; Iain MacKay of Beauly; Margaret MacKay of Newtonmore; John MacLeod of Breakish, Skye; Charles Rose of Torridon.

Iseabail C. MacLeod
Iain A. MacLeod
January 1984

Grammar

Detailed discussion of the complexities of Gaelic grammar is beyond the scope of this guide, but a few sample words are given in various forms to give some idea of why words are found in different spellings.

Initial, internal and ending changes are all used in Gaelic to indicate plural, feminine, genitive case etc. Thus:

Noun	Singular	Plural	Genitive singular	Genitive plural
càrn *masc.*	**an càrn** (the cairn)	**na cùirn** (the cairns)	**a' chùirn** (of the cairn)	**nan càrn** (of the cairns)
coire *masc.*	**an coire** (the corrie)	**na coireachan** (the corries)	**a' choire** (of the corrie)	**nan coireachan** (of the corries)
beinn *fem.*	**a' bheinn** (the hill)	**na beanntan** (the hills)	**na beinne** (of the hill)	**nam beann** (of the hills)
creag *fem.*	**a' chreag** (the rock)	**na creagan** (the rocks)	**na creige** (of the rock)	**nan creag** (of the rocks)

Note:

(1) noun with adjective

masculine - **càrn mor** big cairn
feminine - **beinn mhor** big hill

(2) In Gaelic the adjective usually comes after the noun, but you will find quite a few exceptions to this among Munro names.

Glossary

In order to give some help with the translation of other hill-names, we have compiled a short and therefore highly selective list of common place-name elements, classified into groups. These appear in maps and others sources in many different forms. Some are variant Gaelic spellings but many are produced by different levels of anglicization; we have included, in brackets, a very few of the more widely-used of these variations. We have also given a few plural and genitive forms which are unrecognizably different from the nominative.

Types of hill and other hill names

Gaelic has many words for different types of hill, some of which require an English phrase to translate them - see **meall, màm, stob** etc. below. In the list of names we have rendered most of them as 'hill' or 'peak'.

aonach a mountain ridge; a hill, a moor.
beinn (ben) a hill, mountain.
binnean, binnein a high, pointed hill; a peak.
càrn (cairn) a cairn, heap of stones; a hill of this shape.
cnap a little hill (literally, a knob, lump).
cnoc (knock) a hillock, smallish hill.
creag (craig) a rock; a crag.
cruach a stack-shaped hill (literally, a heap, stack).
màm a large rounded hill (literally, a breast).

meall a rounded hill (literally, a lump).
monadh (mon, mont, mount, mounth) a hill, mountain; a moor; a range.
sàil a rounded hill (literally, a heel).
sgòr(r), sgùr(r) a sharp rocky hill or rocky peak; (of Norse origin).
stac a steep, conical hill; (of Norse origin).
stob a pointed hill (literally, a stake, pointed stick).
stùc(hd) a little hill jutting out from a larger hill; a peak; a cliff, precipice; a steep conical rock; (of Norse origin).
tom a small rounded hill; a piece of rising ground.
tòrr a steep conical hill or mountain; a prominent, steep rock.
tulach a hillock, smallish hill.

Other features

achadh (ach) a field.
allt (ault) a burn, stream, small river.
bàrr a top, summit.
bealach a pass.
bidean a peak, summit.
blàr a plain.
bràigh an upper part; a slope, brae, top.
bruach a bank (of a river, etc); a slope; a border; an edge.
cadha a narrow pass; a narrow ravine; a steep hill, a steep place.
clach a stone.
coire a corrie (literally, a cauldron, kettle).
diollaid a saddle.
druim a ridge (literally, the back (of a person or animal)).
eas a waterfall; (note: *easan* may mean either "waterfalls" or "a little waterfall").
gleann a glen, a narrow valley.
làirig a pass.
leac a flat stone, slab.
leitir a steep slope; the side of a hill (usually one sloping down to the sea or to a loch).
linne a pool.
mullach a summit, top.
sloch(d) a hollow, a pit.
spidean = **bidean.**
sròn a jutting ridge; a peak; a headland (literally, a nose).
toll a hole; a hollow; a crevice.
uamh a cave.

Colours

Gaelic divides the colour spectrum differently from English. For instance the same word **gorm** is used to describe both grass and the sky; it is usually translated as blue. Similarly **glas** is sometimes translated as grey, sometimes as green.

bàn white, light-coloured; fair (of hair or complexion).
buidhe yellow.
dearg red.
donn (dark) brown.
dubh black.
fionn white, pale-coloured.
geal white.
glas grey, greenish-grey, green.
gorm blue; (of grass, foliage etc) green.

liath grey, bluish-grey.
odhar fawnish brown (usually translated as dun-coloured).
riabhach brindled, greyish.
ruadh red, brownish red, red-brown.
uaine green.

Other adjectives

àrd high.
beag (beg) small.
boidheach beautiful.
breac spotted, speckled.
cam crooked.
caol narrow.
ceathach misty.
cruinn round.
eagach notched, indented.
fada long.
garbh rough.
geàrr short.
leathann broad.
maol bald, bare.
mor big.
tarsuinn transverse, (a)cross.

Other common elements
Animals and birds

agh (plural **aighean**) a hind; a heifer.
bò a cow.
calman a dove.
crodh cattle.
cù (plural and genitive singular **coin**) a dog.
damh a stag; an ox.
each (plural and genitive singular **eich**) a horse.
eilid a hind.
eun (plural and genitive singular **eoin**) a bird.
fiadh a deer.
fitheach a raven.
gabhar a goat.
iolair an eagle.
laogh a calf; a deer-calf.
madadh a dog; a wolf; a fox.
muc a pig.
sionnach a fox.

Plants

beithe birch.
caorann rowan, mountain ash.
còinneach moss.
darach oak.
fraoch heather.
giuthas Scots pine.
iubhar yew.
raineach fern, bracken.

Miscellaneous

àiridh a shieling, summer pasture.
bodach an old man.
cailleach an old woman.
coille a wood.
crìoch a boundary.
deas south.
doire a thicket; a clump of trees.
ear east.
frith a deer-forest, i.e. a stretch of land reserved for deer-stalking, in modern times not usually tree-covered.
fuaran a well; a spring.
gaoth wind.
iar west.
meadhon middle.
sìdh, sìth (shee) a fairy hill.
tuath north.
uisge water.

Phonetic Key

The phonetic script used here is based on English spelling and it is therefore impossible to give more than a very rough approximation of the Gaelic sounds, which are quite different from those of English. But it should enable users to pronounce the names in such a way that they would at least be understood by a Gaelic speaker.

Gaelic pronuciation differs from area to area and it is not possible to cover regional variations here. Therefore you may hear quite different pronunciations in some places as well as anglicized versions. The more common of the latter we give as "usually pronounced..."; see, for example, Braeriach.

Note that the key is based on standard Scottish pronunciation and not on standard Southern English. For example, 'day' and 'road' have simple vowels and not diphthongs. Note also that 'r' is always pronounced.

Bold type indicates the stressed syllable.

Where there might be confusion we have used a hyphen to separate syllables.

Vowels

a	as in less**e**r
a	as in t**a**p
aa	as in f**a**ther
ay	as in **day**
e	as in r**e**d
ee	as in d**ee**d, w**ea**k
i	as in t**i**p
Y	as in b**y**
o	as in t**o**p
u	as in b**u**t
oa	as in r**oa**d
aw	as in b**aw**l
oo	as in p**oo**l
ow	as in **ow**l
oi	as in b**oi**l
oe	approximately the sound in French **oeu**f or German **Ö**sterreich.

Consonants

Most of the consonants represent *approximately* the same sounds in English. Note the following:

g as in **g**et
s as in **s**it
y as in **y**et

ch as in lo**ch**; this is pronounced by putting the tip of your tongue on the back of your lower teeth, narrowing the gap at the back of your throat using your tongue and exhaling through this gap to make a sound without using your vocal chords.

gh has no equivalent in English; it is a voiced ch (i.e. it is pronounced like 'ch', but using the vocal chords).

d and t are pronounced with the tip of the tongue touching the back of the lower teeth (and not the teeth ridge as in English).

b is often transcribed as p although the sound is actually somewhere between these two sounds in English, but somewhat closer to p: similarly d is often transcribed as t and g as k.

Sources

1. Books on place-names

Ellice, E C *Place-Names of Glengarry and Glenquoich and their associations,* London 1931

Forbes, A R *Place-Names of Skye and adjacent islands,* Paisley 1923

Gillies, H C *Place-Names of Argyll,* London 1906

Johnston, J B *The Place-Names of Scotland,* Edinburgh 1903

MacBain, A *Place-names Highlands and Islands of Scotland,* Stirling, 1922

Mackay, W *Gaelic Place Names of Upper Strathglass,* 1968

MacKenzie, W C *Scottish Place-Names,* London 1931

Nicolaisen, W F H *Scottish Place-Names,* London 1976

Place names on maps of Scotland and Wales, Ordnance Survey 1968, reprinted with corrections 1981

Stewart, T F *Hill Names of Perthshire,* 1974

Watson, W J *The History of the Celtic Place-Names of Scotland,* Edinburgh 1926

Watson, W J *Place-Names of Ross and Cromarty,* 1904, reprinted 1976

2. Dictionaries

Dwelly, E *The Illustrated Gaelic - English Dictionary,* 1901-1911, now published by Gairm Publications, Glasgow.

MacLennan, M *Gaelic - English and English - Gaelic Dictionary,* Edinburgh 1925, reprinted 1979 by Acair, Stornoway and Aberdeen University Press.

Meaning and Pronunciation of Munros and Tops

The following list is in alphabetical order as in the Index to Table I (p. 67). Each mountain is indicated by its Section number and number within Section of Table I. For example (s4-12) means mountain 12 in Section 4 of Table I.

The names are quoted mainly in the spelling in this present edition of *Munro's Tables* and, where relevant, we have also given the Gaelic on which these are based (and in rarer cases, the common anglicized version where the Tables use the original Gaelic). Many names in the Munro list are not in their correct Gaelic form and we have only given the correct version in a few cases where it might be helpful.

We have translated most names for hill simply as 'hill' or 'peak' although in many cases the words have a more specific meaning—see first section of the glossary (p. 116). Sometimes, for clarity, we have used a possessive form in English (i.e. 'of the') where the Gaelic does not in fact have a genitive. For example *Stob Coire nan Lochan* is strictly 'peak corrie of the small lochs', but we have translated it as 'peak of the corrie of the small lochs'.

A' see next word.

Achaladair, Beinn (s2-36) [bYn acha*lata*r] from the settlement name which, according to W J Watson, is from early Celtic, meaning field of hard water.

Aighenan, Beinn nan (s3-10) [bYn n*a*n Y*a*n*a*n] **aighenan** is probably a variant of **aighean** meaning of the hinds.

Airgiod Bheinn (s6-6) [arikit vYn] silver hill.

Alasdair, Sgùrr (s17-17) [skoor a*lasta*r] Alexander's peak; named after Sheriff Alexander Nicolson, a Skyeman, first person known to have climbed it (1873).

Alder, Ben (s4-62) from the Alder Burn which, according to W J Watson, is from old Gaelic **alldhobhar** rock water.

Alligin, Beinn - Sgùrr Mhor (s13-4) [bYn aalig*a*n - skoor **voar**] **Alligin** is from the name of the settlement (itself originally from the stream name); meaning obscure, but may be from **ailleag** a jewel; **sgùrr mhor** is big peak.

Am, An see next word.

Aonach air Chrith (s10-28) [oenach ayr **chree**] trembling hill.

Aonach Beag (s4-26, 54) [oenach **bayk**] little hill.

Aonach Eagach (s3-21, 39) [oenach **aykach**] notched ridge.

Aonach Meadhoin (s11-8) [oenach mee*a*n] middle hill.

Aonach Mor (s4-23) [oenach **moar**] big hill.

Aosda, Càrn (s6-21) locally known as [kaarn **oesh**] probably **Càrn Aoise** hill of age.

Attow, Ben see **Fhada, Beinn**

Avon, Ben (s8) (name given to the whole mountain) usually called [ben **aan**] from the river name, probably Gaelic **athfhionn** the bright one.

Ballach, Càrn (s9-19) [kaarn **balach**] possibly from Gaelic **ballach** (high-)walled; spotted, speckled or else from **bealach** a pass.

Bàn, Càrn (s9-18) [kaarn **baan**] light-coloured hill.

Bàn Mor, Càrn (s4-26) [kaarn baan **moar**] big light-coloured hill.

Bàn, Sgùrr (s13-15, s14-10) [skoor **baan**] light-coloured peak.

Bàn, Stob (s4-15, 40) [stop **baan**] light-coloured peak.

Banachdich, Sgùrr na (s17-10) [skoor n*a* ba**nachteech**] meaning obscure; according to A R Forbes, may be smallpox peak, from the pitted appearance of some of its rocks; but perhaps from **banachdag** a milkmaid.

Basteir, Am (s17-3) [*a*m bast*a*r] meaning obscure; not, as sometimes supposed, likely to be from **bàsadair** an executioner.

Beinn, Beinn a' etc, **Ben** see next word.

Bhac, Càrn (s6-14) [kaarn **vachk**] peat-banks cairn.

Bhàn Sgòrr (s3-49) [skor **vaan**] light-coloured peak.

Bhàrr, Meall a' (s2-4) [myowl *a* **vaar**] hill of the top or summit.

Bhealaich Dheirg, Sgùrr a' (s11-7) [skoor *a* vyaleech yer*a*k] peak of the red pass.

Bheithir, Beinn a' (s3) (name given to the whole mountain) [bYn *a* **vayhir**] hill of the thunderbolt.

Bheòil, Beinn (s4-63) [bYn **vyawl**] hill of the mouth

Bhinnein, Càrn (s6-19) [kaarn veeny*a*n] pinnacle hill.

Bhreac, Beinn (s8-39) [bYn **vrechk**] speckled hill.

Bhrotain, Beinn (s8-17) [bYn vroht*a*n] hill of the mastiff.

Bhruaich Leith, Stob a' (s3-18) [stop *a* vrooeech lay] peak of the grey bank.

Bhuic, Sgùrr a' (s4-28) [skoor *a* **vooichk**] peak of the roebuck or he-goat.

Bhuidhe, Beinn (s1-7) [bYn **vooee**] yellow hill.

Bhuidheanach Bheag, A' (s5-7) [*a* voo*a*nach **vayk**] the little yellow place.

Bhùird, Beinn a' (s8-48) [bYn *a* **voort**] hill of the table; original Gaelic was **Beinn Bòrd** hill of the tables.

Bhùiridh, Meall a' (s3-26) [myowl *a* **voo**ree] hill of the bellowing (of the stags).

Bidean an Eoin Dearg (s12-21) [beety*a*n *a*n yawn **dye**r*a*k] red peak of the bird.

Bidean nam Bian (s3-33) normally referred to as [bidee*a*n]; probably a corruption of Gaelic **Bidean nam Beann** [beety*a*n n*a*m **byown**] peak of the mountains.

Bidein a' Choire Sheasgaich (s12-23) [beety*a*n *a* chora **hays**geech] peak of the corrie of the barren or milkless cattle.

Bidein a' Ghlas Thuill (s14-12) [beety*a*n *a* **ghlas** hil] peak of the greenish-grey hollow.

Binnein, Stob (Stobinian) (s1-21) usually pronounced [stobiny*a*n] either from Gaelic **binnean** a peak or from **innean** an anvil.

Binnein Beag (s4-2) [beeny*a*n **bayk**] small peak.

Binnein Mor (s4-3) [beeny*a*n **moar**] big peak.

Blà Bheinn (s17-23) [blaa **vY**n] usually called **Blaven** [blaav*a*n] perhaps Old Norse **blà** blue + Gaelic **bheinn** a hill; or perhaps warm hill.

Bodach, Am (s3-42, s4-11) [*a*m **bo**tach] the old man.

Braeriach (s8-8) usually pronounced [bray**ree***a*ch] but known locally as [brY**ree**ach]; Gaelic is **bràigh riabhach** [brY**ree***a*vach] brindled, greyish upper part.

Bràigh Coire Chruinn-bhalgain (s6-7) [brY kor*a* **chroe**-een val*a*kan] slope above the corrie of the little round bag.

Breac, Sgùrr (s14-24) [skoor **brechk**] speckled peak.

Broad Cairn (s7-16) English name.

Bròige, Stob na (s3-30) [stop n*a* **braweek**a] peak of the shoe.

Bruach na Frìthe (s17-5) [broo*a*ch n*a* **free**a] slope of the deer-forest.

Buachaille Etive Beag (s3) (name given to the whole mountain) [boo*a*chil etiv **bayk**] small herdsman of Etive (Gaelic **Eite** [**ayt**a]).

Buachaille Etive Mor (s3) as above with **mor** [moar] big.

Buidhe, Meall (s2-11, 39,. s8-6, s10-13) [myowl **boo**ee] yellow hill.

Bynack Beg (s8-30) [bYnak **bayk**] meaning obscure; possibly from Gaelic **beinneag** a little hill or **beannag** a little band, a kerchief, a cap + **beag** little.

Bynack More (s8-29) [bYnak **moar**] as above with **mor** big.

Cabar, An (s15-2) [*a*n **kap**ar] the antler.

Cac Càrn Beag (s7-20) [ka **kaarn bayk**] **cac** is from **cadha** a steep place; thus, little steep place of the cairn.

Cac Càrn Mor (s7-21) as above with **mor** [moar] big.

Cadha Gobhlach, Stob (s14-20) [stop kah*a* **goa**lach] hill of the forked ravine.

Caillich, Creag na (s2-23) [krayk n*a* **kal**yeech] rock of the old woman.

Caim, Càrn na (s5-6) [kaarn n*a* **kYm**] cairn of the curve.

Cairn Bannoch (s7-12) [kayrn **ban***a*ch] possibly peaked hill or may be from Gaelic **bonnach** a cake.

Cairn Gorm (s8-24) usually pronounced [kayrn **gorm**] Gaelic **Càrn Gorm** [kaarn gor*a*m] blue hill.

Cairn Lochan (s8-26) [kaarn **lo**chan] little-loch hill.

Cairn of Claise (s7-6) usually pronounced [kayrn *a* **glash**a] Gaelic is **càrn na claise** [kaarn n*a* **klash**a] hill of the hollow.

Cairn of Gowal (s7-14) known locally as **Cairn o' the Gowal**; from Gaelic **gobhal** a fork.

Cairn Toul (s8-12) usually called [kayrn **tool**] Gaelic **càrn an t-sabhail** [kaarn *a*n **tow***a*l] hill of the barn.

Cairnwell, The (s6-20) from Gaelic **Càrn Bhalg** hill of the bags (referring to its lumpy shape).

Caisteal (s4-33) [**kas**tyal] castle.

Caisteal, An (s1-14) [*a*n **kas**tyal] the castle.

Càrn, Càrn a', see next word.

Càrnach, Sgùrr na (s11-3) [skoor n*a* **kaar**nach] peak of the stony ground.

Ceannaichean, Sgùrr nan (s12-17) [skoor n*a*n **kyaneech***a*n] peak of the merchants or pedlars.

Ceann Garbh (s15-9) [kyown **gar***a*v] rough head.

Ceapraichean, Meall nan (s15-8) [myowl nan **kyapreech***a*n] perhaps from **ceap** a back, a hilltop.

Cearcallach, An (s9-5) [*a*n **kyark***a*lach] the hoop.

Ceathreamhnan, Sgùrr nan, (s11-26) [skoor n*a*n **keroan***a*n] peak of the quarters.

Chabhair, Beinn (s1-13) [bYn **chav***a*r] may be from obsolete Gaelic **cabhar** a hawk.

Chailleach, A' (s9-21, s14-22) [*a* **chal**yach] the old woman.

Challum, Ben (s2-28) Gaelic **Beinn Chaluim** [bYn **chal***a*m] Malcolm's hill.

Chaorachain, Sgùrr a' (s12-20) [skoor *a* **choer***a*chan] may be peak of the little field of the berries; but on older maps it appears as **Sgùrr a' Chaoruinn** hill of the rowan.

Chaorainn, Beinn a' (s8-41, 9-1) [bYn *a* **choer**an] hill of the rowan.

Chaorainn Bheag, Beinn a' (s8-42) [bYn *a* **choer**an vayk] little hill of the rowan.

Chaorainn, Creag a' (s11-20) [krayk *a* **choer**an] rock of the rowan.

Cheathaich, Beinn (s2-31) [bYn **cheheech**] misty hill.

Chìoch, A' (s11-14) [*a* **chee***a*ch] the breast.

Chlachair, Beinn a' (s4-59) [bYn *a* **chla**char] stonemason's hill.

Chlaidheimh, Beinn a' (s14-11) [bYn *a* **chlY***a*v] hill of the sword.

Chlamhain, Càrn a' (s6-4) [kaarn *a* **chlaa**van] hill of the buzzard.

Chleibh, Beinn a' (s1-8) [bYn *a* **chlayv**] hill of the creel or chest.

Chnò Dearg (s4-45) [chnaw **dyer***a*k] red nut; but the name appears on older maps as **Cnoc Dearg** [krochk **dyer***a*k] red hill.

Chochuill, Beinn a' (s3-8) [bYn *a* **cho**chil] hill of the hood or shell.

Chòinneach, A' (s8-31) [*a* **choa**nyach] the moss.

Chòinneach Mhor, A' (s13-13) [*a* **choa**nyach voar] the big mossy area.

Chòinnich, Sgòr (s4-50) [skor **choa**nyeech] moss peak.

Chòinnich, Sgùrr (s12-22) [skoor **choa**nyeech] moss peak.

Chòinnich Beag, Sgùrr (s4-30) [skoor choanyeech **bayk**] little peak of the moss.

Chòinnich Mor, Sgùrr (s4-29) [skoor choanyeech **moar**] big peak of the moss.

Choire, Sròn a' (s9-8) [srawn *a* **chor***a*] jutting peak (literally, nose) of the corrie.

Choire a' Mhàil, Stob (s4-13) [stop chor *a* **vaal**] peak of the corrie of the rent or tax.

Choire Bhoidheach, Càrn a' (s7-25) [kaarn *a* chor*a* **vaw**yach] hill of the beautiful corrie.

Choire Claurigh, Stob (s4-36) [stop chor*a* **klow**ree] **claurigh** is probably from Gaelic **clamhras** brawling, clamouring.

Choire Dhomhain, Stob a' (s11-42) [stop *a* chor*a* **ghaw**an] peak of the corrie of the depth, hollow.

Choire Ghairbh, Sròn a' (s10-2) [srawn *a* chor*a* **ghir***a*v] jutting peak (literally, nose) of the rough corrie.

Choire Ghlais, Sgùrr a' (s12-12) [skoor *a* chor*a* **ghlash**] peak of the greenish-grey corrie.

Choire Leith, Meall a' (s2-19) [myowl *a* chor*a* **lay**] hill of the grey corrie.

Choire Leith, Stob a' (s4-37) [stop *a* chor*a* **lay**] peak of the grey corrie.

Choire Mheadhoin, Stob a' (s4-42) [stop *a* chor*a* **vee***a***n**] peak of the middle corrie.

Choire Odhar, Stob a' (s3-22, s10-18) [stop *a* chor **oa***a***r**] peak of the dun-coloured corrie.

Chona Chorein, Sròn (s2-10) [srawn chon*a* **chorin**] probably jutting peak (literally, nose) of the meeting of the corries.

Chonzie, Ben (s1-26) locally pronounced [ben **honzay**] but sometimes known as **Ben-y-Hone** [ben ee **hoan**]; according to W J Watson from Gaelic **beinn chomhainn** [bYn **chawan**], the same name as Glencoe (Gaelic **gleann comhann** narrow glen); more probably from Gaelic **chòinnich** [**choa**nyeech] mossy. This would explain the Scotticized spelling, the z representing the Older Scots letter ʒ, which had a y sound.

Chràlaig, A' (s11-12) [*a* **chraa**lik] the basket, creel.

Chrasgaidh, Meall a' (s14-25) [mywol *a* **chras**kee] hill of the crossing.

Chreachain, Beinn a' (s2-38) [bYn *a* **chre**chan] hill of the rock or hill of the clamshell; or perhaps from Gaelic **creach** plunder.

Chroin, Beinn a' (s1-15) [bYn *a* **chron**] hill of harm or danger.

Chroin, Stùc a' (s1-25) [stoochk *a* **chron**] peak of harm or danger.

Chuaich, Meall (s5-5) [myowl **choo***eech] hill of the shallow, two-handled cup (in Scots, **quaich**).

Chùirn, Beinn a' (s2-41) [bYn *a* **choorn**] hill of the cairn.

Churain, Meall a' (s2-33) [myowl *a* **choo**ran] hill of the carrot.

Cìche, Sgùrr na (s10-7) [skoor n*a* **keech***a*] peak of the breast.

Ciste Dhubh (s11-10) [keest*a* **ghoo**] black chest.

Ciste Duibhe, Sgùrr na (s11-4) [skoor n*a* keest*a* **doe**-y*a*] peak of the black chest.

Clach, Stob nan (s2-27) [stop n*a*n **klach**] peak of the stones.

Clach Geala, Sgùrr nan (s14-26) [skoor n*a*n klach **gyal***a*] peak of the white stones.

Clach Leathad (s3-24) usually called [**klach**l*a*t]; Gaelic [klach **l**ehat] stone of the broad slope.

Clachan Geala, Sgùrr nan (s12-4) [skoor n*a*n klachan **gyal***a*] peak of the white stones.

Cloich-mhuilinn, Càrn (s8-18) [kaarn kloich **voo**lin] hill of the millstone.

Cnap a' Chleirich (s8-50) [krahp *a* **chlay**reech] hill of the priest.

Cnap Coire na Spreidhe (s8-28) [krahp kor*a* n*a* **spray***a*] hill of the corrie of the cattle.

Coileachan, An (s14-34) [*a*n **kily***a*chan] the little cock.

Coireachan, Sgùrr nan (s10-6, 10) [skoor n*a*n **kor***a*chan] peak of the corries.

Coire a' Chàirn, Stob (s4-10) [stop kor *a* **chaarn**] peak of the corrie of the cairn.

Coire a' Chriochairein, Sròn (s9-11) [srawn kor*a* **chree***a*char*a*n] possibly jutting peak (literally, nose) of the corrie of the little border keeper.

Coire Altruim, Stob (s3-29) [stop kor **altrim**] peak of the corrie of the fostering or rearing (i.e. where the deer calve and rear their young).

Coir' an Albannaich, Stob (s3-15) [stop kor *a*n al*a*paneech] peak of the corrie of the Scotsman.

Coire an Laoigh, Stob (s4-31) [stob kor *a*n **loe**-ee] peak of the corrie of the calf.

Coire an Lochain, Stob (s1-22) [stop kor *a*n **lochan**] peak of the corrie of the small loch.

Coire an t-Saighdeir, Stob (s8-13) [stop kor *an* t**Y**ty*ar*] peak of the corrie of the soldier.

Coire an t-Sneachda, Stob (s8-27) [stop kor *an* **trachk***a*] peak of the corrie of the snow.

Coire Bhealaich, Stob (s4-27) [stop kor*a* vyaleech] peak of the corrie of the pass.

Coire Cath na Sìne, Stob (s4-35) [stop kor*a* ca n*a* **sheen***a*] peak of the corrie of the battle of the elements.

Coire Choille-rais, Meall (s9-6) [myowl kor*a* chily*a* **rash**] hill of the corrie of the wood promontory; according to W J Watson, from **ros** a promontory.

Coire Dheirg, Stob (s3-13) [stop kor*a* **yer***ak*] red-corrie peak.

Coire Dhuibh, Stob (s9-14) [stop kor*a* **ghoo***eev*] black-corrie peak.

Coire Easain, Stob (s4-32, 41) [stop kor **esan**] peak of the corrie of the little waterfall.

Coire Etchachan, Stob (s8-34) [stop kor **etsh***achan*] Corrie Etchachan peak; see **Etchachan, Càrn.**

Coire Leith, Stob (s3-40) [stop kor*a* **lay**] grey-corrie peak.

Coire Liath Mhor, Stob a' (s13-10) [stop *a* kor*a* **lee***a* voar] peak of the big grey corrie.

Coire Lochan, Stob (s11-41) [stop kor*a* **lochan**] peak of the corrie of the little loch.

Coire Mheadhoin, Càrn na (s11-16) [kaarn n*a* kor*a* **vee***an*] cairn of the middle corrie.

Coire na Ceannain, Stob (s4-39) [stop kor*a* n*a* **kyow**nan] peak of the corrie of the little head.

Coire na Cràlaig, Stob (s11-13) [stop kor*a* n*a* **kraa**lik] peak of the corrie of the basket.

Coire na Fiar Bhealaich, Craig (s10-24) [krayk kor*a* n*a* **fee***a*r vyaleech] rock of the corrie of the slanting pass.

Coire na Gaibhre, Stob (s4-38) [stop kor*a* n*a* **gY***r*a] peak of the corrie of the goat.

Coire na h-Iolaire, Sròn (s4-64) [srawn kor*a* n*a* **hyil***ar*a] jutting peak (literally, nose) of the corrie of the eagle.

Coire na Saobhaidhe, Meall (s7-22) [myowl kor*a* n*a* **soevee***a*] hill of the corrie of the fox's den.

Coire nam Beith, Stob (s3-34) [stop kor*a* n*am* **bay**] peak of the corrie of the birches.

Coire nan Dearcag, Stob (s11-28) [stop kor*a* n*an* **dyar**kak] peak of the corrie of the little berries.

Coire nan Each, Creag (s11-36) [krayk kor*a* n*an* **yach**] rock of the corrie of the horses.

Coire nan Lochan, Stob (s3-35) [stop kor*a* n*an* **lochan**] peak of the corrie of the little lochs.

Coire nan Nead, Mullach (s4-52) [moolach kor*a* n*an* **net**] summit of the corrie of the nests.

Coire Raineach, Stob (s3-32) [stop kor*a* **ran**yach] peak of the fern or bracken corrie.

Coire Sgreamhach, Stob (s3-36) [stop kor*a* **skray**vach] peak of the dreadful or fearful corrie.

Coire Sgriodain, Stob (s4-43) [stob kor*a* **skree***a*dan] peak of the corrie of the scree.

Cona' Mheall (s15-6) usually pronounced [**kon**ival] Gaelic [**kon***a* vyowl] hill of the meeting or joining.

Conbhairean, Sgùrr nan (s11-18) [skoor n*an* **kon***a*varan] peak of the keepers of the hounds.

Con Dhu, Càrn na (s11-33) [kaarn n*a* kon **ghoo**] cairn of the black dog.

Conival (s16-3) see **Cona' mheall.**

Corrag Bhuidhe (s14-18) [korak vooee] yellow finger.

Corranaich, Meall (s2-18) [myowl kor*a*neech] perhaps notched, prickly, hooked or crooked hill, or possibly hill of lamenting.

Craig of Gowal see **Cairn of Gowal**

Creag see next word.

Creagan a' Choire Etchachan (s8-38) [kraykan *a* chor etsh*a*ch*a*n] little rock of Corrie Etchachan; see **Etchachan, Càirn.**

Creise (s3-23) [kraysh] origin unknown.

Crìche, Càrn na (s8-10, s14-29) [kaarn n*a* kreech*a*] hill of the boundary.

Crow Craigies (s7-11) **craigies** is Scots for little rocks.

Cruach Ardrain (s1-18) [kroo*a*ch aardr*a*n] Gaelic probably **cruach àrd-roinn** stack of the high part.

Cruachan, Ben (s3-1) [ben kroo*a*chan] stacky hill.

Cruidh, Meall (s3-12) [myowl krooee] cattle hill.

Cuanail, Meall (s3-3) [myowl koo*a*nal] hill of the flocks.

Cuidhe Crom (s7-23) [koey*a* krowm] crooked wreath (of snow).

Cùl Choire, Stob an (s4-24) [stop *a*n kool chor*a*] hill of the back corrie.

Dail Mhor, Creag an (s8-47) [krayk *a*n dal **voar**] big rock of the river-meadow.

Damh, Creag nan (s10-32) [krayk n*a*n **dav**] rock of the stags.

Dearg, Beinn (s6-3, 15-7) [bYn dyer*a*k] red hill.

Dearg, Càrn (s4-19, 48, 57, s9-16) [kaarn dyer*a*k] red hill.

Dearg Meadhonach, Càrn (s4-22) [kaarn dyer*a*k mee*a*nach] middle red hill.

Dearg, Meall (s3-41) [myowl dyer*a*k] red hill.

Dearg, Sgùrr (s17-13) [skoor **dyer*a*k**] red peak.

Dearg, Stob (s3-2, 27) [stop **dyer*a*k**] red peak.

Derry Cairngorm (s8-36) from Glen Derry, Derry Burn (Gaelic **doire** a thicket).

Devil's Point, The (s8-15) euphemistic translation of **Bod an Deamhain** penis of the devil.

Dhearg, Sgòrr (s3-48) [skor yer*a*k] red peak.

Dhònuill, Sgòrr (s3-47) [skor ghawil] Donald's peak.

Dhubh, Creag (s12-2) [krayk **ghoo**] black rock.

Diamh, Stob (s3-5) probably a mis-spelling of **stob daimh** [stop **dYv**] peak of the stag.

Dìge, Meall na (s1-23) [myowl n*a* dyeek*a*] hill of the moat.

Diollaid a' Chàirn (s4-58) [dyee*a*lat *a* chaarn] saddle of the cairn.

Doire, Stob na (s3-28) [stop n*a* dir*a*] peak of the thicket.

Doire Leathain, Sgùrr an (s10-30) [skoor *a*n dir*a* lehan] peak of the broad thicket.

Dorain, Beinn (s2-34) [bYn doaran] from Gaelic **dobhran;** may be hill of the otter, but more likely hill of the streamlet.

Dòthaidh, Beinn an (s2-35) [bYn *a*n dawhee] hill of the scorching or singeing.

Driesh (s7-19) [dreesh] from Gaelic **dris** a thorn-bush, bramble.

Drochaid an Tuill Easaich (s11-19) [droch*a*t *a*n toe-eel eseech] bridge of the hollow of the waterfall.

Drochaid Ghlas (s3-4) [droch*a*t **ghlas**] grey bridge.

Druim Mor (s7-7) [drim **moar**] big ridge.

Druim Shionnach (s10-27) [drim hee*a*nach] ridge of the fox.

Dubhag, Meall (s8-3) [myowl dooak] hill of the little dark one.

Dubhchraig, Beinn (s1-12) [bYn ˙doochrayk] black-rock hill.

Dubh Doire, Sgùrr a' (s11-25) [skoor *a* **doo** dir*a*] peak of the black thicket.
Dubh-Loch, Creag an (s7-17) [krayk *an* **doo** loch] rock of the black loch.
Dubh Mor, Sgùrr (s17-20) [skoor doo **moar**] big black peak.
Dubh na Dà Bheinn, Sgùrr (s17-21) [skoor doo n*a* daa*v* **Yn**] black peak of the two hills.
Dubh, Sgùrr (s14-9) [skoor **doo**] black peak.
Dubh, Stob (s3-31) [stop **doo**] black peak.
Each, Sgùrr nan (s14-27) [skoor n*an* **yach**] peak of the horses.
Eachan, Beinn nan (s2-22) [bYn n*an* **yachan**] hill of the little horses.
Eag, Sgùrr nan (s17-22) [skoor n*an* **ayk**] peak of the notches.
Ealar, Carn see **Fìdhleir, Càrn an.**
Eas, Càrn (s8-46) [kaarn **es**] waterfall hill.
East Meur Gorm Craig (s8-44) [mayr gor*am*] east blue finger rock.
Eibhinn, Beinn (s4-51) [bYn **ayveen**] delightful hill.
Eich, Sgùrr Creag an (s14-16) [skoor krayk *an* **yaych**] peak of the rock of the horse.
Eididh nan Clach Geala (s15-10) [aydyee n*an* klach **gyal**a] web of the white stones.
Eighe, Beinn - Ruadh Stac Mor (s13-11) (name given to the whole mountain) usually pronounced [ben **ay**] Gaelic [bYn *aya*] file hill. The main summit is **Ruadh Stac-Mor** [roo*agh* stachk **moar**-big red-brown hill.
Eighe, Càrn (s11-40) [kaarn *aya*] file hill.
Eilde Beag, Sgùrr (s4-5) [skoor aylt*a* **bayk**] little peak of the hind.
Eilde Mor, Sgùrr (s4-1) [skoor aylt*a* **moar**] big peak of the hind.
Etchachan, Càrn (s8-23) [kaarn **etsh***ach**an*] Gaelic **eiteachan**, possibly from **eiteach** burnt heather roots.
Eun, Meall nan (s3-16) [myowl n*an* **ayn**] hill of the birds.
Eunaich, Beinn (s3-9) [bYn **ayneech**] fowling hill.
Fafernie (s7-13) [f*a* **fernay**] from Gaelic **feith fearnaidh** bog of the alder place.
Faochagach, Am (s15-5) [am **foech***a*kach] the place of the shells.
Fasarinen, Am (s13-9) [*am* **faas**rin*an*] said locally to mean a path, pass, way through difficult ground.
Fearstaig, Sgùrr na (s12-15) [skoor n*a* **fyar**stak] may be peak of the sea pink or thrift.
Fhada, Beinn (s3-37, s11-23) [bYn *at*a] long hill; s11-23 is often called Ben Attow.
Fhìdhleir, Càrn an (Carn Ealar) (s6-1) [kaarn *an* **yeel**ar] hill of the fiddler.
Fhionnlaidh, Beinn (s3-45, s11-44) [bYn **yoon**lY] Finlay's hill; s11-44 is said to be called after a gamekeeper to MacKenzie of Kintail, known for his violent behaviour.
Fhir Duibhe, Sgùrr an (s13-16) [skoor *an* yeer **doe**-ee] peak of the dark man.
Fhithich, Creag an (s2-13) [krayk *an* **ee**heech] rock of the raven.
Fhuarail, Sgùrr an (s11-9) [skoor *an* **ooa**ral] peak of the coldness.
Fhuarain Mhoir, Meall an (s11-24) [myowl *an* ooaran **voa**-ir] hill of the big well.
Fhuarain, Stob an (s3-44) [stop *an* **ooa**ran] peak of the well.
Fhuaran, Sgùrr (s11-1) [skoor **ooa**ran] not, as generally supposed, peak of the well; local pronunciation is [**ooren**], which must be a different word, of obscure meaning.
Fhuar-thuill, Sgùrr (s12-13) [skoor ooa*r* hil] peak of the cold hollow.
Fiaclan, Càrn nam (s12-19) [kaarn nam **fee***a*chkl*an*] hill of the teeth.
Fiannaidh, Sgòr nam (s3-39) locally **Sgòr nam Fiann** [skor n *an* **fee***an*(ee)] peak of the Fian warriors (followers of Finn MacCoul, hero of Celtic legend).
Fiona, Sgùrr (s14-15) [skoor **fee***an*a] probably from Gaelic **fionn** light-coloured, or perhaps from **fìon** wine. (Pennant in *A Tour in Scotland* (1772) notes: "These crags are called Sgur-fein, or hills of wine").

Fionn Bheinn (s14-35) [fyoon vYn] pale-coloured hill.
Fionn Choire, Sgùrr a' (s17-6) [skoor *a* fyoon chor*a*] peak of the pale-coloured corrie.
Forcan, Sgùrr na (s10-39) [skoor n*a* for*a*k*a*n] peak of the little fork.
Gabhar, Càrn nan (s6-5) [kaarn n*a*n gow*a*r] hill of the goats.
Gabhar, Stob (s3-17) [stop gow*a*r] goat peak.
Gaibhre, Sgòr (s4-49) [skor gYr*a*] goat's peak.
Gàirich (s10-12) [gaareech] roaring.
Gaoith, Sgòr (s8-2) [skor goe-ee] peak of the wind.
Gaor Bheinn (s10-3) usually called **Gulvain** [goolv*a*n], Gaelic [goer vYn]; either from **gaorr** filth, faeces or from **gaoir** noise.
Garbh, Meall (s2-6, 15, 21, s4-46) [myowl gar*a*v] rough hill.
Garbh, Sròn (s11-43) [srawn gar*a*v] rough jutting peak (literally, nose).
Garbh, Stob (s1-19, s3-6) [stop gar*a*v] rough peak.
Garbhanach, An (s4-9) [*an* gar*a*v*a*nach] the rough one.
Garbh Chioch Bheag (s10-9) [gar*a*v chee*a*ch **vayk**] little rough place of the breast.
Garbh Chioch Mhor (s10-8) as above with **mhor** [voar] big.
Geal Chàrn (s4-55, 61, s5-4, s8-7, s9-15) [gyal **chaarn**] white hill.
Gearanach, An (s4-8) [an gyer*a*nach] the complainer.
Ghaordie, Meall (s2-24) locally pronounced [myowl **girday**] possibly from Gaelic **gàirdean** a shoulder, arm, hand.
Ghearrain, Sròn a' (s3-19) [srawn *a* yaran] jutting peak (literally, nose) of the gelding.
Gheoidh, Càrn a' (s6-18) [kaarn *a* yowee] hill of the goose.
Ghlais Choire, Stob a' (s3-25) [stop *a* ghlash chor*a*] peak of the grey corrie.
Ghlas, Beinn (s2-17) usually pronounced [ben **glas**], Gaelic [bYn **ghlas**] greenish-grey hill.
Ghlas Bheinn, A' (s11-22) [*a* ghlas vYn] the greenish-grey hill.
Ghlas-uillt, Creag a' (s7-26) [krayk *a* **ghlas** oo-eelt] rock of the greenish-grey burn or stream.
Ghlo, Beinn a' (s6) (name given to the whole mountain) usually pronounced [ben ay **gloa**]; Gaelic [bYn *a* ghloa] hill of the hood or veil.
Ghluasaid, Càrn (s11-21) [kaarn ghloo*a*sat] hill of movement.
Ghorm a' Bhealaich, Creag (s12-14) [krayk ghor*a*m *a* **vya**leech] blue rock of the pass.
Ghreadaidh, Sgùrr a' (s17-8) [skoor *a* ghraytee] peak of torment, anxiety.
Gillean, Sgùrr nan (s17-2) [skoor n*a*n geelyan] peak of the young men.
Giubhas, Sròn nan (s3-20) [srawn n*a*n gyooas] jutting peak (literally, nose) of the Scots pines.
Glas Bheinn Mhor (s3-14) [glas vYn **voar**] big greenish-grey hill.
Glas Choire, Meall (s4-53) [myowl glas chor*a*] hill of the greenish-grey corrie.
Glas Leathad Beag (s15-4) [glas leh*a*t **bayk**] little greenish-grey slope.
Glas Leathad Mor (s15-1) [glas leh*a*t **moar**] big greenish-grey slope.
Glas Maol (s7-1) [glas **moel**] greenish-grey bare hill; original Gaelic was **Glas Mheall** greenish-grey hill.
Glas, Meall (s2-30) [myowl **glas**] greenish-grey hill.
Glas Mheall Liath (s14-14) [glas vyowl lee*a*] greenish-grey hill.
Glas Mheall Mor (s5-8, s14-13) [glas vyowl **moar**] big greenish-grey hill.
Glas Tulaichean (s6-9) [glas **too**leech*a*n] greenish-grey hillocks.

Gleouraich (s10-23) [**glyaw**reech] possibly uproar, noise.

Gobhar, Càrn nan (s12-1,11) [kaarn n*a*n **gow***a*r] hill of the goats.

Gorm, Càrn (s2-8) [kaarn gor*a*m] blue hill; see also **Cairngorm.**

Gorm, Meall (s14-32) [myowl gor*a*m] blue hill.

Greigh, Meall (s2-16) [myowl **gray**] hill of the horse studs; (horses were pastured there at one time); but also known as **Meall Gruaidh** cheek hill.

Gruagaichean, Na (s4-6) [n*a* groo*a*keech*a*n] the maidens.

Gulvain see **Gaor Bheinn.**

Heasgarnich, Beinn (s2-25) [bYn **hesk***a*rneech] Gaelic **beinn sheasgarnaich;** perhaps from **seasgaireach** sheltering, peaceful or from **seasgach** barren or milkless cattle.

Hope, Ben (s16-4) Gaelic **beinn** a hill + Old Norse **hóp** a bay.

Ìme, Ben (s1-3) [ben **eem**] butter hill; butter was often made at the hill shielings or hill pastures.

Isean, Sròn an (s3-7) [srawn *a*n **ee**shan] jutting peak (literally, nose) of the chicken.

Iubhair, Sgòr an (s4-12) [skor *a*n **yoo***a*r] peak of the yew.

Iutharn Mhor, Beinn (s6-11) [bYn **yoo***a*rn **voar**] not, as sometimes supposed, big hill of hell; perhaps from Gaelic **fhiubharainn** an edge point.

Iutharn Bheag, Beinn (s6-13) as above with **bheag** [vayk] little.

Iutharn, Sgòr (s4-56) [skor **yoo***a*rn] may be peak of hell but see also above.

Klibreck, Ben (s16-5) [ben **klee**brek] Gaelic probably **beinn na cleith bric** hill of the speckled cliff.

Ladhar Bheinn (s10-17) [laa*a*r vYn] hoof or claw hill.

Làirige, Sròn na (s8-9) [srawn n*a* **laar**ik*a*] jutting peak (literally, nose) of the pass.

Laoigh, Beinn see **Lui, Ben.**

Lap, Beinn na (s4-47) [bYn n*a* **lahp**] **lap** means a defective spot in a colour.

Lapaich, Sgùrr na (s11-39, s12-3) [skoor n*a* **lah**peech] peak of the bog.

Lawers, Ben (s2-12) pronounced as in English; according to W J Watson, from Gaelic **labhar** loud (describing the noise of a stream); or possibly from **ladhar** a hoof, a claw. The name has an English plural in reference to the three division of the Lawers district.

Leabaidh an Daimh Bhuidhe (s8-43) [lyepay *a*n dYv **vooee**] bed of the yellow stag.

Leac nan Each, Sgùrr (s10-37) [skoor lyechk n*a*n **yach**] peak of the slab of the horses.

Leacach, Creag (s7-4) [krayk **lyechk***a*ch] slabby rock.

Leth-choin, Creag an (s8-25) [krayk *a*n **lye**-chon] usually known by its English translation, **Lurcher's Crag.**

Leth-chreag, An (s11-47) [*a*n **lye** chrayk] the half rock; may refer to one of a pair of rocks.

Liath, Càrn (s6-8, s9-12) [kaarn **lee***a*] grey hill.

Liath, Meall (s2-3) [myowl **lee***a*] grey hill.

Liath Mhor, Beinn (s13-3) [bYn **lee***a* **voar**] big grey hill.

Liath Mhor Fannaich, Beinn (s14-31) [bYn **lee***a* **voar faneech**] big grey hill of Fannich, which is from the name of the loch (of obscure origin).

Liathach (s13) (name given to the whole mountain) [**lee***a*hach], but locally pronounced [**lee***a*ghach] the grey one.

Lochain, Sgùrr an (s10-31) [skoor *a*n **lochan**] peak of the little loch.

Lochain Uaine, Sgòr an (s8-14) [skor *a*n lochan **ooanya**] peak of the little green loch.

Lochain Uaine, Sgùrr an (s8-37) [skoor *a*n lochan **ooanya**] peak of the little green loch.

Lochnagar (s7) (name given to the whole mountain) [**lochn***a*gaar] called after a small loch high in its north-east corrie - **Lochan na Gàire** little loch of the noisy sound.

Lomond, Ben (s1-1) [ben loam*a*nd] Gaelic **Beinn Laomuinn** [bYn loemen]; according to W J Watson Lomond is from an old Celtic word for a beacon; the name is unlikely to be from the River Leven, Gaelic **leamhan** an elm tree.

Lord Berkeley's Seat (s14-17) English name.

Lui, Ben (s1-9) usually pronounced [ben loo-ee]; Gaelic **Beinn Laoigh** [bYn loe-ee] calves or calf hill.

Luinne Bheinn (s10-15) [loony*a* vYn] perhaps hill of anger, or hill of mirth or melody.

Lurg Mhor (s12-24) [loor*a*k voar] big ridge stretching into the plain.

Macdui, Ben (s8-20) [ben m*a*kdooee] popularly thought to mean the "hill of the black pig" but according to W J Watson, from Gaelic **beinn MacDuibh** either hill of the sons of Dubh (the black one) or MacDuff's hill. (Considerable stretches of land in the area were held at one time by MacDuff, Earl of Fife).

Mairg, Càrn (s2-2) [karn mar*a*k] may be hill of sorrow, pity, folly; or hill of the boundary (from Scots **mark, merk**); or perhaps from Gaelic **marag** a (black) pudding (from its rounded shape).

Màm nan Càrn (s6-12) [maam n*a*n **kaarn**] hill of the cairns.

Màm Sodhail (s11-35) usually called [mam **sool**] Gaelic [maam **soe-al**] hill of the barns.

Maoile Lunndaidh (s12-18) [moel*a* loondY] according to W J Watson *(Place-names of Ross and Cromarty)*, bare hill of the wet place.

Maol Chean-dearg (s13-1) [moel ch*a*n **dyer*a*k**] bald red head.

Maol Chinn Dearg (s10-29) [moel cheen **dyer*a*k**] bald red head.

Mayar (s7-18) [may*a*r] known locally as **the Mayar**; meaning obscure; perhaps from Gaelic **m'aighear** [mY*a*r] my delight, or from **magh** a plain.

Meagaidh, Creag (s9-4) usually called [krayg **megay**] possibly bogland rock.

Meall, Meall a' etc, see next word.

Meikle Pap (s7-24) known locally as **the Muckle Pap** [muk*a*l pap] Scots for big breast.

Mhadaidh, Sgùrr a' (s17-7) [skoor *a* **vatee**] peak of the fox.

Mhaighdean, A' (s14-5) [*a* vYtya*n*] the maiden.

Mhàim, Càrn a' (s8-19) [kaarn *a* vYm] cairn of the large rounded hill.

Mhàim, Creag a' (s10-26) [krayk *a* vYm] rock of the large rounded hill.

Mhàim, Sgùrr a' (s4-14) [skoor *a* vYm] peak of the large rounded hill.

Mhanach, Beinn (s2-40) [byn **vanach**] monk hill.

Mhaoraich, Sgùrr a' (s10-21) [skoor *a* **voereech**] peak or the shellfish.

Mhaoraich Beag, Sgùrr a' (s10-22) [skoor *a* **voereech** bayk] little peak of the shellfish.

Mharconaich, A' (s5-3) [*a* vark*a*neech] probably from **marc** a horse, thus, the horse place.

Mheadhoin, Beinn (s8-32) usually called [ben **vayn**]; Gaelic [bYn **vee*a*n**] middle hill.

MhicChoinnich, Sgùrr (s17-16) [skoor veechk ch*u*nyeech] MacKenzie's peak; named after a well-known Cuillins guide, John MacKenzie.

Mhor, Creag (s2-5, 26) [krayk **voar**] big rock

Mhor, Sgùrr see **Alligin, Beinn**.

Monadh Mor (s8-16) [mon*a*gh **moar**] big hill.

Mor Dearg, Càrn (s4-21) [kaarn moar **dyer*a*k**] big red hill.

Mor, Meall (s12-25) [myowl **moar**] big hill.

Mor, Sgùrr (s10-11, s14-28) [skoor **moar**] big peak.

More, Ben (s1-20, 17-1) usually pronounced as in English; Gaelic **beinn mhor** [bYn **voar**] big hill.

More Assynt, Ben (s16-1) [ben moar assint] from the district name, which is probably from Old Norse **ass** a rocky ridge + **endi** an end.

Moruisg (s12-16) [moarishk] perhaps big water.

Mount Keen (s7-30) known locally as [mun **keen**] from Gaelic **monadh caoin** smooth or pleasant hill.

Mullach an Rathain (s13-7) [moolach *an* raahan] summit of the row of pinnacles; (the 'Horns of Alligin' are sometimes referred to locally as **rathain).**

Mullach Cadha Rainich (s11-38) [moolach kah*a* raneech] summit of the narrow pass of the fern of bracken.

Mullach Clach a' Bhlàir (s8-1) [moolach klach *a* **vlaar**] summit of the stone of the plain.

Mullach Coire Mhic Fhearchair (s14-7) [moolach kor*a* veechk er*a*char] summit of the corrie of the son of Farquar.

Mullach Coire nan Nead (s4-52) [moolach kor*a* n*an* **net**] summit of the corrie of the nests.

Mullach Fraoch-choire (s11-11) [moolach froech **chor***a*] heather-corrie peak.

Mullach na Dheiragain (s11-31) [moolach n*a* yer*a*kan] meaning obscure; perhaps summit of the hawk.

Mullach nan Coirean (s4-16) [moolach n*an* koran] summit of the corries.

Mullach Sìthidh (s11-32) [moolach **sheehee**] fairy summit.

Narnain, Ben (s1-2) usually pronounced [ben **narnayn**] origin unknown.

Nevis, Ben (s4-18); Gaelic **Beinn Nibheis;** from the river name; according to W J Watson, probably from an old Gaelic word meaning venemous.

Odhar, Meall (s7-2) [myowl o*aa*r] dun-coloured hill.

Oss, Ben (s1-11) [ben **os**] loch-outlet hill.

Peithirean, Meall nam (s14-30) [myowl n*am* **pe**hiran] hill of the gamekeepers or foresters or perhaps hill of the thunderbolts.

Pitridh, Creag (s4-60) [krayk **pee**tree] perhaps from the surname Petrie.

Poite Coire Ardair, Stob (s9-9) [stop poty*a* kor **aar**dar] peak of the pot of the high corrie.

Puist Coire Ardair (s9-7) [poosht kor **aar**dar] posts of the high corrie; Corrie Ardair is criss-crossed with fenceposts.

Riabhachan, An (s12-5) [*an* ree*a*vachan] the brindled, greyish one.

Riach, Sròn (s8-22) [srawn **ree**ach] brindled, greyish jutting peak (literally, nose).

Rìgh, Càrn an (s6-10) [kaarn *an* **ree**] hill of the king.

Ruadh, Sgòrr (s13-2) [skoor roo*a*gh] red peak.

Ruadh Stac Mor (s14-4) [roo*a*gh stachk **moar**] big red peak; see also **Eighe, Beinn.**

Ruaidhe, Sgùrr na (s12-10) [skoor n*a* rooY] peak of the redness.

Saddle, The (s10-33) English name.

Sagairt Beag, Càrn an t- (s7-28) [kaarn *an* tak*a*rsht **bayk**] little hill of the priest.

Sagairt Mor, Càrn an t- (s7-29) [kaarn *an* tak*a*rsht **moar**] big hill of the priest.

Saighead, Sgùrr nan (s11-2) [skoor n*an* s**Y**at] peak of the arrows.

Sàil Chaorainn (s11-15) [saal **choe**ran] hill (literally, heel) of the rowan.

Sàil Liath (s14-21) [saal lee*a*] grey hill (literally, heel).

Sàil Mhor (s13-12) [saal **voar**] big hill (literally, heel).

Sàileag (s11-6) [**saal**ak] little hill.

Schiehallion (s2-1) [sheehaly*an*] according to W J Watson, 'the fairy hill of the Caledonians'.

Seana Bhràigh (s15-11) [shen*a* vrY] old upper part.

Sgàirneach Mhor (s5-1) [skaarnyach **voar**] big stony hillside.

Sgarsoch, An (s6-2) [*an* **skar**soch] the place of sharp rocks.

Sgiath Chùil (s2-32) [skee*a* **chool**] back wing.

Sgìne, Sgùrr na (s10-40) [skoor n*a* **skeen***a*] peak of the knife.

Sgòr, Sgòrr see next word.

Sgòr, An (s2-7) [*an* **skor**] the peak.

Sgoran Dubh Mor (s8-5) [skoran doo **moar**] big black peaks. This group of peaks is known as the Sgoran Dubhs and this was considered to be the biggest of them (although it is not in fact the highest).

Sgritheall, Beinn (s10-19) [bYn skreehal] probably scree or gravel hill.

Sgùlain, Càrn (s9-20) [kaarn skoolan] hill of the basket or of the old man.

Sgulaird, Beinn (s3-46) [bYn skoolard] origin unknown.

Sgùmain, Sgùrr (s17-19) [skoor skoo**man**] peak of the (boat) bailer.

Sgùr, Sgùrr see next word.

Slioch (s14-1) [shlee*a*ch] from Gaelic **sleagh** a spear.

Sluichd, Stob an t- (s8-51) [stop *an* **tloo**-eechk] peak of the hollow.

Snaim, Meall an t- (9-13) [myowl *an* **trYm**] hill of the difficulty or of the knot.

Socach, An (s6-16, s11-34, s12-9) [*an* **sochk**ach] the projecting place (from **soc** a beak, snout).

Socaich, Beinn na (s4-34) [bYn n*a* **sochk**eech] hill of the projecting place (from **soc** a beak, snout).

Spàinteach, Sgùrr nan (s11-5) [skoor n*an* **spaan**tyach] peak of the Spaniards; named in memory of the Spanish mercenaries who fought with the Jacobites at the Battle of Glenshiel in 1719.

Spidean a' Choire Leith (s13-6) [speetyan *a* chor*a* **lay**] peak of the grey corrie.

Spidean Coire nan Clach (s13-14) [speetyan kor*a* n*an* **klach**] peak of the stones.

Spidean Dhòmhnuill Bhric (s10-36) [speetyan ghawil **vreechk**] peak of spotted Donald.

Spidean Mialach (s10-25) [speetyan mee*a*lach] **mialach** means lousy but the name may refer to deer or other animals.

Sròn, Sròn a' etc., see next word.

Stacan Dubha (s8-35) [stachkan doo*a*] little black stacks.

Starav, Ben (s3-11) [ben starav] origin unknown.

Stob, Stob a' etc., see next word.

Stobinian see **Binnein, Stob.**

Stùc, An (s2-14) [*an* **stoochk**] the peak.

Stùc Bheag (s11-29) [stoochk **vayk**] little peak.

Stùc Mhor (s11-30) [stoochk **voar**] big peak.

Stùchd an Lochain (s2-9) [stoochk *an* **lo**chan] peak of the little loch.

Tarmachan, Meall nan (s2-20) [myowl n*an* tar*a*machan] hill of the ptarmigans.

Tarsuinn, Beinn (s14-6) [bYn **tar**shin] transverse hill.

Teallach, An (s14) (name given to the whole mountain) [*an* **tya**lach] the forge.

Teanga, Meall na (s10-1) [myowl n*a* **tyeng***a*] hill of the tongue.

Thearlaich, Sgùrr (s17-18) [skoor **hyaar**leech] Charles' peak; named after Charles Pilkington, a member of the Scottish Mountaineering Club.

Thormaid, Sgùrr (s17-12) [skoor **hor***a*mat] Norman's peak; named after Norman Collie, a member of the Scottish Mountaineering Club who did much early mountaineering exploration is Scotland.

Thuilm, Sgùrr (s10-5) [skoor **hoo**lim] peak of the rounded hillock.

Tigh Mor na Seilge (s11-17) [tY moar n*a* **shayl***a*ka] big house of the hunt.

Toll Creagach (s11-48) [towl **kray**kach] rocky hollow.

Tolmount (s7-10) known locally as [toal-**mun**] old Gaelic **dol** a valley + Gaelic **monadh** a hill.

Tom a' Chòinich (s11-45, s15-3) [towm *a* **choa**nyeech] hill of the moss.

Tom a' Chòinich Beag (s11-46) [towm *a* **choa**nyeech bayk] small hill of the moss.

Tom Buidhe (s7-9) [towm **boo**ee] yellow hill.

Tom Dubh (s8-11) [towm **doo**] black hill.

Tom na Gruagaich (s13-5) [towm n*a* **groo***a*keech] hill of the maiden.

Tom na Sròine (s4-25) [towm n*a* **srawn***a*] hill of the jutting ridge (literally, nose).

Toman Còinich (s14-23) [towman **koa**nyeech] little hill of the moss.

Tudair, An (s11-37) Gaelic **an tughadair** [*a*n **too***a*tar] the thatcher.

Tuill Bhàin, Sgùrr an (s14-3) [skoor *a*n **toe-eel vaan**] peak of the pale hollow.

Tuirc, Càrn an (s7-8) [kaarn *a*n **toork**] hill of the boar.

Tulaichean, Beinn (s1-17) [bYn **too**leech*a*n] hill of the hillocks.

Udlamain, Beinn (s5-2) [bYn **oot**l*a*man] according to A MacBain, the source may be either **udlaidh** gloomy, dark, lonely or **udalan** a swivel, a joint; but may be from **uideal** a swinging, an unsteadiness.

Ulaidh, Sgòr na h- (s3-43) [skor n*a* **hool**Y] peak of the treasure.

Vane, Ben (s1-4) usually pronounced as in English; Gaelic **Beinn Mheadhon** [bYn **vee***a*n] middle hill.

Vorlich, Ben (s1-5, 24) [ben **vawr**leech] Gaelic **Beinn Mhur'laig**; according to W. J. Watson, hill of the bay (literally, 'of the sea-bag').

West Meur Gorm Craig, (s8-45) [mayr **gor***a*m] west blue finger rock.

White Mounth (s7) (name given to the whole mountain); usually pronounced [munth]; from Gaelic **monadh** a hill.

Wyvis, Ben (s15) (name given to the whole mountain); [ben **wi**vis] locally [**wee**vis]; Gaelic **Fuathas**; perhaps hill of terror.